P9-CBJ-228
L. Nemec

The Great and Little One of Prague

By the Same Author

Kult Krista Boha A Kult Cisaru V Antickem Svete (1940)

The Episcopal and Vatican Reaction to the Persecution of the Catholic Church in Czechoslovakia (1953)

Annunciation of the Blessed Virgin Church in Its Golden History 1905 - 1955 (1955)

Church and State in Czechoslovakia (1955)

The Cult of St. Jude Thaddeus in Czechoslovakia (1956)

The Infant of Prague (1958)

Spiritual Treasury of the Holy Child of Prague . . . (Manual and Prayerbook, in Preparation)

The Great and Little One of Prague

By

LUDVIK NEMEC

The Peter Reilly Co.
131 North Thirteenth Street
Philadelphia, Pa.

Nihil Obstat

REV. RICHARD GINDER, M.A., S.T.L.

Censor Librorum

Imprimatur

✠ JOHN WRIGHT

Bishop of Pittsburgh

November 17, 1959

Library of Congress Catalog Card Number 59-15897

MANUFACTURED IN THE UNITED STATES OF AMERICA

To my friend,
Sister M. Adele Whaley,
Sisters of St. Joseph, Baden, Pennsylvania
gifted writer and scholar
whose continuing interest and generous assistance
has been an invaluable help in my work.

PREFATORY NOTE

The unhappy history of Prague, never more sad than in the first half of the present century, would make the very thought of that venerable city one of great sadness for sensitive Christians were it not for its association with the cult of what Paul Claudel has called "the eternal Infancy of God," symbolized by the popularly-beloved Infant of Prague.

Indeed, such has been the gentle influence of devotion to the Infant of Prague in millions of Christian homes all over the world that when most of the devout hear the name of Prague, they think, in their simplicity, of the radiant image of a royal child, the Infant of Prague, rather than of the harrowing chapters of a tragic city's political and military misfortunes.

It is good that at a moment when counsels of despair for the future of Eastern Europe and the Faith there are so widespread, we should think of the Divine Infant, still enshrined in the midst of the faithful of Prague, as a hostage to hope that the eternally new spirit of God will renew the battle-scarred face of the earth and bring to new birth the ancient spiritual fervor of a holy corner of the Christian world.

Father Nemec has performed a work of both patriotism and piety in bringing together so much of the history, lore and poetry of the devotion which originated in a corner of Christendom that he knows and loves well. He documents every aspect of that devotion which, originating in Prague, has spread to every land where people pray to God, in Christ, with the childlike faith that is the sure key to Heaven.

Those who already love the Infant of Prague will here find further reasons for their favorite devotion. Those who, in their sophistication, are less impressed, will be struck, perhaps, by the place of the Infant in the spirituality and poetry of the French diplomat and intellectual who was Paul Claudel. The striking account of this unexpected appeal of the Infant of Prague is one of the most interesting contributions of Father Nemec's book and will, one feels sure, open up to many readers new insights into the spiritual and theological depths of a devotion which not a few have esteemed largely sentimental.

✠ John Wright

Bishop of Pittsburgh

July 6, 1959

PREFACE

Devotion to the Holy Child of Prague, it seems profitable to emphasize, appeals strongly to man's reason, heart, and sentiments. It inspires the comprehension of humility and littleness as the requisite for attaining to the ultimate end of the spiritual life. It also provides a sensible form which is the outward expression of the concept contained within the devotion. Even the few who see something sentimental in the devotion must eventually be held by its universal appeal as they come to the realization of the spiritual and theological principles underlying this devotion. The historic promise itself, as the keystone of the devotion is in too much accord with reason to be considered sentimental, for it is a concomitant of Divine worship: to give glory to God and to hope for graces in return.

It is the author's aim to present the devotion to the Holy Child of Prague in such a way as to elicit that understanding of the spiritual concept indicated by the title of the book: *The Great and Little One of Prague*. This idea is reflected in the rich symbolism of the representation as it appears on the jacket of this book. The young Pittsburgh artist, John Leo Baker, has succeeded in depicting the Infant as the King of nations and the universe, with the clear inter-relation of the Cross and Crown. Simultaneously it appears in the portrayal of the Infant dressed in the historic Chinese robes, a gift from the Carmelite nuns in Shanghai in 1896, which bears embroidered in Chinese characters along the hem of the garment the following words: "Divine Infant Jesus have mercy on China; return it to the faith and free it from the power of the evil spirit." Along the sleeves is woven the prayer: "Jesus, Divine Child, Thy kingdom come in China." This motif of suffering China supplements the symbolism and forms a fitting background for the Holy Child - the King offering to bless all those in need.

In order to help crystallize this idea, numerous illustrations are contained within the work giving direction to those who are truly desirous of grasping the real meaning of the Kingship of the Holy Child. The reader will find a rich source of information pointing to the indisputable fact that the Infant desires to be honored. There is beauty in the devotional hagiology contained in the story about the miraculous statue as it was found, forgotten, neglected, damaged, repaired, and finally enthroned in glory.

The first part of the book is an attempt to unveil some of the artistic representations which show the development of the Holy Child - the King, as it first appeared in the sixteenth century and became fully symbolized in the Infant of Prague in the seventeenth century. It is beyond the scope of this work to consider all the details attendant upon artistic portrayals, rather it is the author's intention to concentrate on the Holy Child - the King in its historic steps to the royal entre of the Infant of Prague.

The second part of the book contains detailed events connected with the royal entrance of the Infant of Prague on the historic scene. In order to be as exact as possible, the author presents for the first time an English version of the first story ever written about the Infant, *Pragerisches Gross und Klein* of 1737, composed by the Carmelite Father, Emmerich of St. Stephen, of Prague. Thus the reader not only has the satisfaction of an entirely reliable account, but also the convincing assurance that the importance of the devotion rests on historical accuracy, and should be accepted as providential without any doubt or hesitancy. Available to anyone wishing to read the account from the original German text are four photostatic copies provided by the author from a microfilm of the original in Charles University library in Prague. These may be had from the Library of Congress, The Catholic University of America library, Washington, D. C., Duquesne University library, Pittsburgh, St. Procopius College library, Lisle, Illinois, while a microfilm may be had from the Sisters of St. Joseph Archivium, Baden, Pennsylvania. Before these presentations this material was not available anywhere in the United States.

The direction of this work shows how the devotion really developed from the original mystical communication of its first promoter, the Discalced Carmelite, Father Cyril of the Mother of God, with the miraculous statue, to its ecclesiastically approved and enthusiastically accepted form of public devotion. In order to best accomplish this, the author transferred Emmerich's narration into English in order to satisfy the complete literary and devotional needs of the reader. A realization of the difficulty involved in the task of the transition from the old German text with its eighteenth century expressions into modern English idiom, and at the same time preserving all the flavor of the devotional taste to be found in its original inspiration, makes this work an important literary contribution, whose historical value is that of a valuable source.

The third part of the book gives a wider view to the development of devotional events with an emphasis on modern and contemporary literary documents up to the present time, thus completing an over-all historical picture. The concise style of the material should help the reader to view the history of the devotion as it is presented in an easy-to-read essay form, profitable to both the scholar and the general reading public, both deriving from it inspiration.

Ludvik Nemec

Feast of Christ the King, 1959

ACKNOWLEDGMENTS

I wish to express my sincere gratitude to the following persons:

His Excellency, John J. Wright, Bishop of Pittsburgh, for his kindness in writing the Prefatory Note; Sister M. Adele Whaley, M.A., of the Sisters of St. Joseph of Baden, Pennsylvania for constructive criticism of the manuscript and reading galley and page proofs; Sister Vincent Ferrer Clifford, S.S.J., Baden, Pennsylvania, for typing the manuscript and helping to index; Mrs. Marie Carney of Pittsburgh for typing material; John Leo Baker, Pittsburgh, for his artistic elaboration of an original representation of the Infant as it appears on the book jacket; Miss Elizabeth Dafflinger, Pittsburgh, for making available to the author her rich collection of Madonnas with Infants; Suzanne Silvercruys Stevenson, for permission to reproduce her representation of the Infant; James J. Metcalfe, for permission to reprint his poem, *O Infant Jesus of Prague*.

Furthermore, I hereby make a general and public acknowledgment to all the authors and publishing houses that are cited in the references of this book.

CONTENTS

PART ONE

PART TWO

PART THREE

CHAPTER 1

THE DIVINE CHILD IN ART

"And the Child grew, and waxed strong, full of wisdom; and the grace of God was in Him." (Luke 2:40) With this brief record, St. Luke covers that important period of life which lies between infancy and the twelfth year; and yet, brief as it is, it clearly illuminates a vital truth.[1] Growth is the keyword of the passage. Growth is a wonder and glory of all childhood. Growth was the beautiful secret of the childhood of Jesus.[2]

Jesus thought as a child while He learned His letters and began to read in the Holy Scriptures at His mother's knee. He felt as a child as he wandered and played with His little cousin, John, in the flowering fields of Galilee. He spoke as a child while He walked with Mary and Joseph, or sat in the carpenter shop, helping a little and hindering a little the work, and bringing into the daily life of the laboring man that innocent and uplifting charm that comes from companionship with a boy.

There does not appear to have been anything sudden or startling in the development of His childhood. It went forward gradually and imperceptibly. He did not leap from infancy to maturity magically. He grew up to it through long and slow beautiful years, through the wonder of awe at new thoughts dawning with every morning, and new affections deepening with every evening, and a soul enlarging under the silent influence of grace.

To visualize such a growth of happy childhood to the boyhood of Jesus, it is not necessary to consider the many legends gathered in the apocryphal books, which are mere inventions; they give us no real help in completing the outline of Christ's childhood. Much more helpful are the interpretations of art, which are rich and full of meaning. No part of the gospel history has been more abundantly and beautifully illustrated in art than this verse of St. Luke, which tells us in a word how quietly the life of Jesus unfolded in the home of Nazareth.

In numerous masterpieces of art one can find good ground for believing that the Child Jesus, living in a devout Hebrew household in a little town of Nazareth, must have enjoyed the blessings characteristic of childhood. We have an evidence of this in the eight distinct names used in the Hebrew language to mark the different periods of a child's growth. All the traditions of the race were in favor of the sanctity of the home, and their Holy Scriptures hallowed it by the authority of Jehovah Himself.

Moreover, it was a happy circumstance that this home of the holy family was in Galilee. For although that northern province was despised by the inhabitants of Jerusalem, life there was far more free and natural than it was in Judea. Galilee was fair and smiling. The vine and the olive flourished here; the rabbis held it was easier to rear a forest of olive trees in Galilee than one child in Judea.[3]

The simplicity of the Galilean life must have been favorable also to those pleasures of human relations that are tasted most perfectly by children free from care. The warmth and devotion of His friendship reveals a heart that did not grow reserved in early solitude. A natural companion of His boyish pleasures would be His cousin, the child of Zachary and Elizabeth, afterwards known as John the Baptist. Artists have no apology to make for so often depicting the Child Jesus and John playing together with the lambs and birds, beside flowing streams.

The education of the Child was not neglected, for on this point the Jewish law was strict. Religion was the chief factor in education, and doubtless it was begun by the mother, who would explain to her son the fascinating stories of the Old Testament, while she held Him, listening, in her arms. She would teach Him passages of Scripture to recite from memory. And we may confidently say of Jesus, as St. Paul said of his disciple, Timothy, that "from a child he knew the Holy Scripture." (2 Tim. 3:15)[4] All these circumstances of the life of the Holy Child have been woven by the artists into their thoughts of the childhood of Christ.

Such representations in art are helpful for the better understanding of the "glory hidden in humility," related in the gospels. The works of art which depict the subject are almost innumerable, and to review the Divine Child in art throughout the centuries is difficult, because of the diversity of motifs, schools, and media developed through the ages. Since the mystery of the Incarnation of the Divine Word was a subject of prime interest to all Christendom, it is easily understandable that the Infancy of Jesus was one of the most popular subjects in all art.[5]

It will be helpful to consider various types of representations of the Blessed Mother, such as the *Ave Maria,* the *Mater Amabilis,* the *Mater Dolorosa,* and the *Regina Coeli.*[6] However, the *Mater Amabilis* — the young mother with the Infant Jesus — is of particular interest to us because of the restricted scope of our subject, the infancy and boyhood of Jesus.

Beginning with Christian art in the catacombs, one can follow its development of the Infancy throughout the centuries, selecting examples from the different periods, such as Byzantine, Roman, Gothic, Renaissance, Baroque, Rococo, Pseudo-Classical, and Modern.

Early art portraying the Infancy was not developed as fully as we might expect because the subject was overshadowed by the Passion of Our Lord, and because the subject itself, surprisingly enough, is seldom mentioned in the Gospels.

The first authentic representation of the Virgin and Child in art is a fresco found in the Catacomb of St. Priscilla of the second century, a seated figure of the Virgin, her head partially covered with a short veil, with the Infant in her arms. Nearby stands a man clothed in the pallium, holding a volume in one hand, the other pointing to a star above the two figures. The man represents the prophet Isaias, and the star symbolizes the divinity of Christ.[7]

There are third century lunettes of the Virgin seated with the Infant. One, depicting two Magi, is to be found in the cemetery of Saints Peter and Marcellinus.[8] In the cemetery of St. Domitilla, we find another, with four Magi.[9] The Epiphany is also depicted on circular plates of the fourth century and in medals of the fifth.[10]

Representations of the Nativity and the Adoration of the Magi were greatly multiplied during the fifth and sixth centuries.[11] A much disputed Madonna, greatly beloved by the people of Rome, is known as the *Salus Populi Romani.*[12] According to tradition it was painted by St. Luke, and is considered to be one of the oldest known images of the Blessed Virgin with the Infant.[13]

From the fourth to the fourteenth centuries, artistic emphasis centered in Constantinople, producing many evidences of Byzantine art. The best known is the Madonna of Divine Wisdom,[14] in which Constantine offers his city and Justinian presents his church, built in 537, to the Blessed Mother for her protection. Another well-known icon is Our Lady of Vladimir,[15] taken by Vladimir from Constantinople to Kiev in 1155, and placed in the Cathedral of the Assumption in Moscow at the end of the fourteenth century.

While Greek art flourished in the East, mosaicists were still working in Rome, and have left us fragments of their work. One of the oldest was recently rediscovered in the Church of Saint Francis of Rome, when Pico Cellini, an expert restorer, was called in to clean what was believed to be a nineteenth century work. Underneath was hidden a Madonna of the thirteenth century, which in turn covered one from the fifth century.[16]

Other fragments from the seventh and eighth centuries are in Rome. A Madonna and Child, an elaborate mosaic of the ninth century, is in the Chapel of St. Praxedes. In this mosaic Our Lady is seated on a throne with the Infant on her lap, His little arms extended in blessing.[17]

A new impetus was given to painting in the West by Giovanni (960) and Petrolino (1100). To our regret, they left nothing of their efforts. A great revival of art started under Cimabue (1240-1302), often called the father of modern painting. Cimabue and his protegé, Giotto di Bordonne, known as Giotto (1276-1377) and the latter's pupils, the Biotteschi, comprise the earliest of Florentine painters. While adhering in many ways to the Byzantine, they changed that style, introducing flesh tones, and making dress less rigid. Examples of this development are Cimabue's *Madonna and Child* in the Louvre, Paris,[18] and Giotto's *Life of the Virgin* in the Scrovigni in the Church of the Arena, Padua.[19]

Frà Angelico (1387-1455), the portrayer of mystic illumination,[20] was the last great painter of the Middle Ages and the first of the Renaissance. His tranquil attitudes, fresh colors, and delicate tints are evident in all his works, especially in his *Madonna of the Holy Conversation,* in the Monastery of St. Mark, Florence. This gives us, as a detail, the loveliest Christ Child in all art.

Leonardo da Vinci (1452-1519), the one man whose talents were to influence painters of all times, was born fifty years after Masaccio (1402-1428), the pioneer of the realists and founder of the Renaissance period. A master of design, harmony and color, Da Vinci has left us several Madonnas, the best known of which is his *Madonna of the Rocks,* painted in Milan betwen 1482 and 1499.

Da Vinci founded the Lombard school, of which Antonio (Allegri) Correggio (1494-1534) was the outstanding pupil and successor to Raphael Santi (1483-1520), the founder of the Roman school and one of the world's greatest painters. Raphael has left us approximately fifty Madonnas, about thirty-five of which have been catalogued in public collections. Of these, the two outstanding are his *Alba Madonna,* National Gallery, Washington, D. C.,[21] whose delicate coloring personifies his love of beauty for its own sake; and his *Sistine Madonna,*[22] his last and finest, recently returned by the Russians, who removed it during World War II from the Dresden Gallery in Germany, where it had been since 1761. This Madonna is considered the ideal of all womankind; it is the epitome of power, beauty and love. Correggio's *Madonna Adoring the Child,* originally in the Uffizi Gallery, Florence, and much copied on Christmas cards today, exemplifies his delineation of happy children, whose attitudes are as expressive as their faces.

Giovanni Bellini (1426-1516) often called the father of Venetian painting, has produced more pictures of the Virgin and Child than any other painter.[23] His *Virgin Adoring the Child,* now in the National Gallery in London, was one of his favorite subjects.

Tiziano Vecellio, known as Titian (1477-1576), world-beloved for his *Assumption of the Virgin* and called the creator of modern painting, has left us a few Madonnas including that of the *Madonna of the Rabbit* in the Louvre.

Jacopa Robusti (1512-1594), known as Tintoretto, from the trade of his father, "Il Tintoret," the dyer, has left us a Nativity scene from his Life of Christ, which may be found in the School of San Rocca, Venice.[24]

The Flemish school, which flourished from the fourteenth to the eighteenth centuries, included such well known artists as the Van Eycks, Van der Weyden, Memling, Matsys, Bril, Breughel, Rubens, Snyders and Teniers. Most Flemish artists have left Madonna and Child pictures. Outstanding, however, is the work of Peter Paul Rubens (1577-1640), *The Return of the Holy Family from Egypt,* which portrays the Blessed Mother and St. Joseph with Jesus as a young child accompanying them. God the Father is represented as watching over them from above. Another interesting work of this period is Hans Memling's (1425-1495) *Virgin with the*

Apple, in which the Blessed Mother, symbolic of the second Eve, presents the apple to the Child.

The art of Albrecht Dürer (1471-1528) done during the German Reformation period combined renaissance and medieval style. Both elements are represented in his *Festival of the Rosary,* now in the Gallery of the Monastery of Strahov, in Prague.[25] His life of the Virgin, in wood cuts, a Madonna in Dresden, and *Jesus Among the Doctors,* in the Bernerini, Rome, are of particular interest.

Spanish art expanded during the Inquisition. It was sombre in tone, intense in ideals, and spiritually austere. El Greco, Domenico Theotocopuli (1545-1614), a native of Crete, who adopted Toledo as his home as he was in turn adopted and accepted by all Spain,[26] portrays his faith in the human spirit striving heavenward. His *Holy Family,* in the Cleveland Museum of Art, done in the baroque style, depicts the happy family life, with the Virgin taking fruit from a bowl held by St. Joseph, and presenting it to the Child Jesus.

The best known and most beloved of all Spanish painters is Bartolomeo Esteban Murillo (1618-1682), beloved for his *Immaculate Conception.* He has left us several versions of the Madonna of the Rosary, where the Virgin is teaching the Infant Jesus to pray. Two pictures are in the Prado, Madrid, representing a Holy Family, in which the young Jesus holds a bird aloft in his right hand, teasing his tiny dog upon the floor. A Madonna with the Infant Jesus, assisted by an angel distributing bread, is in the Budapest Museum of Fine Arts.

The French School flourished continuously from the Italian Renaissance at the time of Francis I through the classical, romantic, realistic, impressionistic, and post-impressionistic periods, and had given us numerous Madonnas. For our purpose, however, we select the *Madonna of the Grapes* by Pierre Mignard (1610-1695) as representative of the school, because of its soft, high coloring, and its air of vivacity; and we select the *Holy Family* by Nicholas Poussin (1594-1665) in which the little St. John tries to take the Infant Jesus from the lap of His Mother as she bathes Him. The first painting hangs in the Louvre; the second in the Fogg Museum of Harvard University.

Previous to the seventeenth century, most of the art of England was imported, but much of it was destroyed by the reformers of the sixteenth century and the Puritans of the seventeenth century. A few of the surviving pictures[27] include the *Adoration of the Magi,* formerly in Winterbourne Dauntsey Church, Wilts, and a Madonna and Child in Winston Church, Suffolk.

Since the Finding of the Child Jesus in the Temple is the culmination of the divine childhood, it is of special interest to note that this scene appears very often, depicted by many of the masters as "Christ Among the Doctors." This has been expressed in modern art by two admirable pictures. One of them is Holman Hunt's, *The Finding of the Saviour in the Temple.* The other is the picture by Professor Heinrich Hofmann in Dresden.[29]

The tradition of ecclesiastical art in the United States survives in carved and painted figures of the Madonna and Child in altarpieces in the Sangre de Cristo Mountains north of Santa Fe, brought there originally by the early Spanish missionaries. During the past quarter century, religious art has been rapidly developing in this country, one example being Geri Melchers' *Madonna of the Rappahannock* in the Richmond Art Gallery, Virginia. Unique in style, the Madonna appears in modern costume with a straw hat on the table beside her. This may have been adapted from the *Divine Shepherdess*[30] by Miquel Tovar, 1704, in which Our Lady, dressed in sheepskin, wears a large straw hat decked with roses. John Singer Sargent has left us a Madonna and Child in his Nativity scene, one of the fifteen mysteries of the Rosary painted on the walls of the Public Library in Boston, Massachusetts.

Contemporary artists have produced many Madonna and Child pictures, all of equal worth.[31] A few oustanding ones are the *Madonna of the Sioux,* a painting by Brother Bonaventure of the Priests of the Sacred Heart for the Indian mission school in Chamberlain, South Dakota; and the mural of the Madonna in Our Lady Chapel of St. Bernard Church, Pittsburgh, Pennsylvania, the work of Jan Henryk de Rosen, assisted by the young talented artist, John Leo Baker of Pittsburgh, designer of the jacket of this book.

Apropos of the relationship of theology and art, a general review will show that seldom is the Child Jesus depicted alone in the interim between His birth and His appearance among the Doctors of Law in the Temple of Jerusalem. This is quite understandable when we realize that a child of tender years is constantly in the care of his mother. Nevertheless in the artist's conception of mother and child, attention is always focused on the Child, without whom even the greatest Madonnas would lose their importance.

We have endeavored to give in this brief review of the Madonna art of the ages reasonable proof of ever-flourishing devotion to the Divine Infancy. Conspicuous by its absence is any depiction of the Infant or the Boy Jesus as Christ the King. This we present as further evidence that artistic concepts correlated directly with the development of theological views. Hence because the theological synthesis of the Divine Child-King evolved at a later date, we can look for its artistic presentation not earlier perhaps than the fifteenth century. There are, for example, the famous *Ara Coeli* image of the Child-King in Rome (1480); the *Santo Niño* of Cebu in the Philippines (1521); the *Santo Bambino* of Salerno (1600); and others of later date. But the majority of Child-King art belongs to the nineteenth and twentieth centuries. Artists, like theologians, needed time to develop the Divine Child-King thesis; they found it difficult to represent a King through the medium of a helpless child in the crib of Bethlehem.

A modern approach made by the Czech artist Nicholas Ales has depicted the divine Child in the crib, attended on either side by St. Procopius and St. John Nepomucene, with St. Wenceslaus directly behind, in the act of crowning the Infant. By such a composite the artist tried not to disturb the traditional lines between the Infant of Bethlehem and Christ the King, hoping to combine both characters in the same depiction.[32] In so doing, of course, he found it necessary to sacrifice the presence of the Virgin Mother Mary.

It has been pointed out, not without significance, that the slowness of art to represent the Divine Child-King is all the more remarkable from the historical fact of the popularity of the adoration of the Magi as a subject beloved through all the Christian centuries. Noticeable, too, in another popular subject — the finding of the Child in the Temple — is the fact that Christ, here exercising a magisterial office, nevertheless hides His royal character. Yet centuries before, the writings of the prophets of Israel proclaim Him the Messias, and the King of all the nations of the world.

CHAPTER 2

THE HOLY CHILD OF PRAGUE

The profile of the Infant of Prague presupposes that we become acquainted with the historic background of the statue and how it made its appearance in Bohemia. As a result of the Thirty Years' War, Prague in the seventeenth century was a scene of turmoil. Here where a confluence of interests: religious, cultural, political, and economic, had heightened and embittered the waters of unrest, the Infant Jesus brought once again his plea for peace among men of good will. In fact the accidents of time and place would seem to point out the fundamental lesson to be learned in a period of heretical reformation and self-assertive renaissance as one of need for child-like humility. "A little child shall lead thee."[1] A conviction of this truth would stem the growing circles of seventeenth century egocentrism that were threatening to reject the theocentric needs of universal man of every age.

The Infant King prepared His way many years before in Spain. Behind the public scenes of history, the Carmelite mystic, St. Teresa of Avila, had cultivated among her followers an intimate and tender devotion to the humanity of Christ the King.[2] Discalced and calced Carmelites like the Venerable Francis of the Child Jesus had perpetuated the age-old tradition of love for the Divine Infant in their Carmels, preparing the world for His advent beyond Spain and Europe to the East, and also to the Americas and the Western world. Since the mysteries of the God-King were first penetrated in Spain, it was seemly, therefore, that Spain was the stage for a wedding gift which was the first step by which the Infant transposed His image into Bohemia and to the world.

Maria Manriques de Lara of the celebrated Spanish family of Mendoza stands at the cradle of the history of the Infant of Prague. For it was she who brought the statue from Spain to Prague on the occasion of her marriage in 1556 to Lord Vratislav Pernstyn, a leader in the social and political life of the Czech Kingdom.

How the statue originally came into the possession of Maria has been the subject of many theories. One theory is that Maria obtained it from St. Teresa of Avila, who first conceived the idea of dressing the Infant as a king. Another theory, and a more credible one, is that it was a wedding gift to Maria from her mother Isabella. Although many legends are related to this event and are used for the explanation, their basis is not established in historical fact. Yet the idea of a family heirloom transferred to a bride on the occasion of her departure for a foreign land is reasonable, since such a memento would help to bridge the gap soon to separate her from loved ones.

The marriage of Maria Manriques de Lara and Lord Vratislav produced twenty children, seven of whom reached maturity. Of all the children, Polyxena was her mother's favorite. Like her mother, she possessed great religious zeal. Through marriage she was able to direct this zeal to combating heresy in high places. Her first marriage to William Rosenberg, the Supreme Burgrave of Bohemia, placed her in the upper strata of European society. Zdenek Adalbert Lobkowitz was his worthy successor in marriage with this noblewoman.

Princess Polyxena, though beautiful, was not the fragile type. Historians praise her bravery in rescuing and secretly harboring Martinic and Slavata during the de-fenestration of imperial officials in 1618.[3] For this act she and her son, Wenceslaus, were imprisoned and penalized by having her property confiscated. Her husband's life was spared because he had been traveling abroad, and only through a decree of Ferdinand II on August 17, 1624 was the family honor "reinstated" and a restoration made of their freedom and property.

Upon the death of her mother, Polyxena came into possession of the family estate and heirlooms, which included the statue of the Holy Child. Historians are uncertain as to the exact date, but this probably occurred in 1608. Following the death of her second husband, she assumed the duties of directing the affairs of the family estates for her son, and acting as legal guardian for the children of her deceased brother John. During such a time of responsibility, it was natural for her to entreat the help of the Infant. This same devoutness moved her to donate this precious possession to the Discalced Carmelites in Prague. And so in 1628 the statue was placed in permanent residence in a shrine that was to become one of the most famous in the world.

A glimpse at the homeland of the Infant reveals that the history of the present Czechoslovakia began to take form in 863 with the arrival of Saints Cyril and Methodius, whose missionary efforts brought the present country into close relations with the East. But during their subsequent development, Bohemia, Moravia, and Silesia — the so-called historical provinces of St. Wenceslaus Crown — turned to the West and were eminently successful in acquiring its culture. Slovakia was torn from this great Moravian empire as early as 906. All these countries were part of the Austro-Hungarian empire until 1918, when they were unified under the name of Czechoslovakia.

Prague, proclaimed the mother of cities and the princess of provinces, had been the center of the political life of Czechoslovakia and the seat of its episcopal see since the tenth century. Located in the very heart of the continent of Europe, its stones testify to a troubled past, to conflicting ideas over religion and its impact on human society. Her art treasures, most of them churches, or the embellishment of these churches, bear silent testimony to this fact.

The church that is of prime interest to us is that of Our Lady of Victory. For it is here that the miraculous statue of the Infant of Prague is preserved. In its artistic character and ecclesiastical history, this church characterizes certain influences which mark the Renaissance and the Baroque as eras where very definite values of religion and life were integrated. This edifice, originally known as the Church of the Blessed Trinity, belonged to the Lutherans until after the battle of White Mountain (1620). In 1624 Emperor Ferdinand II gave this church to the Discalced Carmelites, who were newly introduced to Prague.

The Image of the Infant of Prague is enshrined at the center altar on the Epistle side of the Church of Our Lady of Victory. It rests in a marble niche between statues of the Blessed Mother and St. Joseph. The first sight of the image may present an unusual and perhaps startling appearance. To appreciate its appeal one must forget momentarily the ideal of Christian art that has for centuries placed an Infant, tender and warmly human, in a manger bed in Bethlehem, embraced with loving eyes by Mary and Joseph. There is more of the Epiphany here than the traditional nativity scene. The Infant of Prague, eighteen inches tall, is the miniature model of a king in regal robes. His left hand holds a sphere, the image of the world, surmounted by a cross. There is dignity beyond childhood in the manner of his pontifical blessing. The right hand extends two fingers to symbolize His divine and human natures; the thumb and last two fingers touch, symbolic of the Father, Son and Holy Spirit in the mystery of the Holy Trinity, the focal point of Christian faith. A closer look at the fingers shows two jeweled rings. These are the gifts of a nobleman and his wife, who donated them in gratitude for the miraculous cure of their young daughter. The image itself is of wood covered with wax. The wig of blond human hair is a comparatively modern detail. During the baroque era the image wore a white wig after the fashion of the day. The crown, at first sight unproportional to the size of the body, was added later with much ceremony by an official of the Czech kingdom named Bernard Ignatius Martinic. (1655.) The Sacred Name is spelled out in precious stones on the pedestal below the image.

The royal robes of the Infant King are patterned after the vestments worn by a priest on liturgical occasions. The innermost garment is made of linen, tunic-style, resembling the alb. The next robe is lace; covering these is a vestment, usually of silk or velvet, covered by a miniature cape. These vestments are changed periodically to correspond to the liturgical seasons. At present there are thirty-nine sets of garments in the collection. These were donated by the faithful in gratitude for favors received. One highly prized for its age and historic value is the set of green velvet, the gift of Empress Maria Theresa on a visit to Prague. The original ones are preserved in a special repository in the sacristry.

We have restricted ourselves to this profile of the Infant, knowing that the reader will find full information pertaining to the miraculous statue and shrine in the translation following. There and in the third part, dealing with the modern history of the Infant, one will appreciate the basis of the world-wide devotion to the Great and Little One of Prague.

CHAPTER 3

COMMENTARY ON THE TRANSLATION

It is with a deep sense of satisfaction that we introduce for the first time an English version of the oldest story ever told about the Infant of Prague. It is the work of Father Emmerich of St. Stephen, entitled *Pragerisches Gross und Klein,* compiled and published in 1737 by this German Carmelite from the records of Venerable Father Cyril of the Mother of God, through whose efforts the Infant was made known to the world as a Child-King.

The presentation of this first English version has literary significance in that only a few copies of the German original and its Czech edition are extant, none of them available in the United States. The library of Charles University in Prague owns both the German edition *Pragerisches Gross und Klein* (1737), and the Czech edition of 1749. Our present translation was made from the German text of a reprint published in 1760.[1]

Through the courtesy of Dr. Jan Petrmichl, director of Charles University library, the German edition was microfilmed and sent in May of 1955 to the late Father Augustine Studeny, O.S.B., of St. Procopius Priory in Chicago, Illinois, who subsequently placed it at the author's disposal. The facilities of Duquesne University, Pittsburgh, Pennsylvania, made possible a photostatic copy of this material, from which the present critical English version was produced.

Its significance is further emphasized by the fact that later historians treated *Pragerisches Gross und Klein* in such a way that authenticity of detail and accuracy of historical background suffered thereby. It is this consideration mainly, the need for reliability, that has prompted the author to reproduce from its original source a sound account in English. Convinced of its value to English-speaking people, I hope that the present text will enrich their literature by providing an historically interesting document, one that will also prove instrumental in furthering the already widespread devotion to the Infant of Prague.

First it may be helpful to present a biographical sketch of its authors: Father Cyril of the Mother of God, the first promoter of the devotion, and Father Emmerich of St. Stephen, its zealous propagator and the narrator of the story of *The Great and Little One* that is unfolded in the seventy-five "chapters" or episodes of Part II. Father Cyril is not an author in the professional sense of the term, but he provided the records on which Father Emmerich based his account. As early as 1636 a poem entitled "Das Prager Lied" (Song of Prague) was in public circulation. The fact that it appears as late as 1806 in the anthology *Des Knaben Wunderhorn,* edited by Achim von Arnim and Clemens

Brentano, is an indication of long-lived popularity. The anonymous "Song of Prague" presupposes an apostle of extraordinary zeal. It is not improbable the Father Cyril was its author.

Little is known of Father Cyril of the Mother of God (1590-1675), who promoted this devotion in its earliest stages. He was born Nicholas Schockwilerg[2] on January 2, 1590 at Luxemburg. He entered the Carmelite Order at an early age, was ordained a priest in 1624, and was later elected a Prior. Spiritually restless, affected deeply by the forthcoming reforms of the Order and motivated by a desire for greater personal perfection, Father Cyril left his monastery in 1628 to enter the more austere Discalced Carmelites in Prague. Having completed his novitiate here in 1629, he professed his solemn vows on October 28, 1630 in Munich, Bavaria, where he spent the next seven years. The remainder of his years were passed in Prague. After his death on February 4, 1675, he was buried in the catacombs beneath the Church of Our Lady of Victory in Prague.

The fame of Father Cyril lies in his complete dedication to the cause of promoting devotion to the Infant Jesus, so that the statue which originally stood in a small niche in a novitiate oratory eventually came to be enthroned in a magnificent church of world-wide fame. In his "Prayer to the Infant Jesus of Prague,"[3] now translated into many languages, we are given a more satisfactory picture of this Carmelite monk than we could gain from a whole volume of panegyrics. It both sums up his aspirations and points out his sanctity.

But the Lord who tries His chosen ones put to the test this particular soul, to render him worthy of the apostolate to which he was called.

On Christmas eve of 1629, after the celebration of a Solemn High Mass, Father Cyril asked permission of the Prior to remain a while longer in the novitiate chapel, where the Infant appeared to be smiling. Disturbed in spirit almost to the limit of endurance, he threw himself at the feet of the image and entreated the Infant once again, with all the ardor of his heart, to have compassion on his miserable soul. Could the Divine Heart remain insensible to such fervent pleadings?

Such was the effect of his fervent prayer that every cloud of doubt, of aridity, of spiritual suffering immediately vanished from the heart of Father Cyril. His soul became suffused with a joy that radiated from his countenance, and was urged on to heights of spiritual perfection.[4] In such a manifestation of grace, the Holy Infant was preparing an indomitable crusader of His cult among a Christian population.

Subsequently, in 1630, Father Cyril left the monastery at Prague for Munich. At this time, bitter warfare was being waged throughout all Bohemia. Prague was invaded by the Huguenots. One can easily imagine Father Cyril's deep distress in having to abandon his small treasure, namely, the statue of the Holy Infant. But because this sacrifice had been asked by obedience, he promptly submitted himself to the wishes of his superiors.

Seven years of catastrophe and suffering passed. On the feast of Pentecost, 1637, the religious war having ended, the pious monk was summoned back to Prague by his superiors. His first thought was to search for the image so dear to him, but to his great dismay, he discovered it among the debris. Saddest of all was the condition in which it was found — its arms broken, the vestments filthy. Nevertheless, he embraced it, cleaned it as best he could, and replaced it on the novitiate altar, where it became an object of great devotion for the entire community.

One day the divine Infant spoke to Father Cyril, who had been kneeling at His feet in fervent prayer: "Have mercy on Me, and I will have mercy on you! Give Me back My Hands and I will grant you peace! The more you honor Me, the more will I favor you." The words re-echoed reprovingly. But how could the statue be repaired when the monastery was so impoverished? With misgivings he approached his superior on the subject, and the response given can be readily guessed. Nothing was done about the restoration. Three days later Father Cyril was called to the bedside of a dying nobleman who offered him a hundred florins for the necessary repairs on the statue. Unfortunately, however, the Prior used the donation to purchase a new statue. On the very day of the installation, the statue fell and crumbled into fragments, providing a sign of God's disfavor.

"Place me at the entrance to the sacristy; whoever comes there will take pity on me," pleaded the Infant once again to Father Cyril. His heart filled with new confidence, the monk did not hesitate this time. Very soon afterwards there approached the sacristy entrance a stranger, on business with the prior. He remarked about the damaged condition of the statue there, and offered to stand the personal expense of having it repaired.

This occurred in 1639, and from that year on, there are many wonderful things on record concerning the miraculous image. Father Cyril's notes are filled with references to the promise: "The more you honor Me the more will I bless you." He was the first to witness the gradual fulfillment of this promise, and was deeply distressed one day to discover the statue missing from its pedestal. An inner voice assured him, however, that the loss was temporary; the statue would be recovered and the sacrilege repaired. When summoned to the bedside of a sick person needing spiritual help, he learned there the circumstances of the theft. After a brief reprimand to its "abductor" he brought back the missing treasure.

It was Father Cyril's privilege to erect the first chapel in honor of the Infant, directed to do so through an apparition. The monk was absorbed in the mystery of the Incarnation on the vigil of the Immaculate Conception, when a light attracted his attention to the ceiling of the choir. Out of a mystic cloud there he discerned the figure of Our Lady, enclosing a space with her upraised arms, as if to indicate the place she approved for a shrine. When he hurried outside to the indicated spot, Father Cyril found the outlines of a building. What was there the barest sketch became a beautiful reality through the financial help of the Lobkowitz family.

His first chapel shrine completed, the Infant was translated on the morning of the feast of the Holy Name of Jesus, 1644, attended by white-robed monks and devotees among the faithful. None was more jubilant than Father Cyril himself. He had seen realized, one after another, his cherished expectations of advancing the cause of the Holy Infant. Practically speaking, his apostolate could be said to have reached its end with this dedication ceremony, but the venerable promoter was to live to see another solemn triumph. This took place the following Easter at a pontifical mass, when Bishop de Corti paused after the Offertory prayers to raise the jewel-embedded gold crown from the altar to the head of the image enshrined above. This royal event as described by Father Emmerich recalls a promise of God to those who partake in His worship in the words of the historian of the first Book of Kings: "He who has given Me glory will also be glorified by Me."

Looking back on Father Cyril's apostolate, these words can be read almost as prophecy of the honor due this faithful servant of the Infant. In fact many persons today who entreat the Infant for some particular favor confidently seek it through the intercession of Venerable Cyril of the Mother of God, and feel consoled at reciting the special prayer he composed.

The list of remarkable events traceable to the shrine of the miraculous image at Prague extends through a century after its restoration by Cyril. During this time, devotion to the Infant gathered spiritual momentum, so to speak, sufficiently great to push beyond the limits of Prague to the whole Christian world. Psychologically this force was impressive enough to sustain the devotion even during the period of political and religious strain that witnessed its semi-eclipse during the nineteenth century.

The second outstanding apostle of this devotion was Bernard Joseph Barat, born February 23, 1691 in Raab. The religious name by which this Carmelite is better known is Emmerich of St. Stephen.[5] His religious profession on August 10, 1709 was the successful end of a novitiate training begun in 1709, in a Carmelite minor seminary in Prague, where there was early evidence of the novice's deep spiritual insights. Once he became outstanding in philosophical and sacred studies, Father Emmerich brought renown to his Order as a writer and orator. Proud of his successes, the Carmelite superiors gave full approval and their blessing to his plan to direct literary efforts in extending devotion to the Infant of Prague. Specifically his main ambition was to collect and edit the manuscripts left in the monastic archives by Father Cyril of the Mother of God. These he would edit along with a number of contemporary writings, including his own, and create a glorious symposium in writing dedicated to the honor of the Great and Little One of Prague. What finally came of this zealous design was this impressive volume entitled and subtitled in the lengthy manner typical of the eighteenth century:

Pragerisches Gross und Klein Das ist: Geschichts Verfassung, des in seinen seltsamen gnaden, schlinbaren Wunder Zeichen, Wunder wurdigen Begebenheiten, Grossen: In seiner aus Jungfrau Wachs gestalten Heiligen Bildnuss, Kleinee: Kindleins Jesu. Welches schon uber hundred jarr bey denen Barfüssigen Carmelitern in der Königl. Kleiner stadt Prag andachtigst verehret wird. Zusammen getragen mit eingemensten sinn-und Lehreichen Concepten aus der Heil. Schrift ordentlich beschrieben: Deme bey gefügt seynd die Tag-Zeiten und Litaney vom Heiligsten Nahmen Jesu.

Its seventy-five chapters can be viewed today as a treasured part of the archives in Our Lady of Victory archives in Prague under the title *Memorial Book.* The Emmerich text is a 1737 publication by Adam Floeder. The book was enthusiastically received, as evidenced by the rapid distribution of the first thousand copies. A second run of two thousand followed in 1740. Its Czech edition, titled *Prazské-Weliké a Malé* was published by Frank Hladky, this time in seventy-three chapters, without noticeable deletion of essential material. The Italian edition came out in Trent in 1750, eight years after Father Emmerich of St. Stephen had left Prague to take up residence in Vienna. There, from the vantage point of Definitor of the Carmelite Order, he could feel gratified to view the expansive results of his dedicated zeal. At his death in 1756 eulogists pointed to a career distinguished above all by service to the Infant-Kingship of Christ.

In preparing *Pragerisches Gross und Klein* we were constantly aware of the problem of how to preserve the flavor of the original German in terms concurrent with the modern English idiom. This is mainly a matter of semantics and style with which all translators of necessity must reckon, with varying degrees of success. Because the text is laden with biblical allusions, we found it helpful to consider the advice given by Hilaire Belloc, which we quote in excerpt:

> Translate boldly: render the sense by the corresponding sense without troubling over the verbal difficulties in your way. Where such rendering of sense by corresponding sense involves considerable amplification, do not hesitate to amplify for fear of being verbose. . . . Sometimes, even, a whole passage must be thus transmuted, a whole paragraph thrown into a new form, if we would justly render the sense of the original; and the rule should stand, that after having grasped as exactly as possible all that the original stands for, with the proportion between its various parts, the distinction between what is emphasized and what is left on a lower plane, we should say to ourselves not "How shall I make this foreigner talk English" but "What would an Englishman have said to express the same?" This is translation. That is the very essence of the art: the resurrection of an alien thing in a native body; not the dressing it up in native clothes, but the giving to it of native flesh and blood.[6]

It is important for the reader to bear in mind that the Emmerich text is an adaptation of the records made by Father Cyril of the Mother of God (1590-1675). Within the scope of its many brief chapters, there is noticeable a lack of names and other documentary evidence we have come to consider requisite for the careful historian. Such omissions are understandable if one remembers that Father Cyril was a confessor of souls, and more than once reveals both his care to insure the sacramental seal of confession and a natural deference to omit anything that might embarrass the persons involved. Father Cyril, moreover, was much more the mystic than the crusader in his approach to devotion to the divine Infant. It remained for Father Emmerich to translate the characteristic *quod Deus vult* of his predecessor in the apostolate into more militant terms. Read in this way the translated text speaks plainly of the oratorical style of Father Emmerich's day. A modern ear more attuned to dispassionate speech can be somewhat offended on this point, judging the writer as one lacking in moderation, frequently constraining to his own purpose a biblical parallel, and this, without benefit of documentation. This objection, such a critic will hold, takes on more significance from the fact that Father Emmerich was more the scriptural scholar than the historian. But the author's aim, let us agree, was not only to inform but also to edify his readers within the hagiological conventions of his time. If their mystical overtones disturb the modern ear, the Emmerich stories are not for this reason to be discredited.[7] Critics attached by tradition and personal preference to less ornate modes of speaking are here given a taste of the baroque style with the added historical interest that the narrative content reflects a definite response to the spiritual revival that was then holding fort against the inroads of a militant heresy.

On the other hand, certain readers may commend the spiritual awareness of Father Emmerich to have seen some innermost meaning of the Scriptures that helped him to make clear a point of Christian teaching, and so promote holiness of life among his hearers. Or, those more enlightened about the demands made of modern Catholic exegetes, may object that Emmerich at times prefers some figurative meaning to the literal meaning of the sacred text. Such critics may discern in his turn of words a conscious straining after some effect other than the simple expounding of the divine word, and they may even impute to his frequent application of sacred text to story something less than the care and dignity that Scripture demands in exposition. But in fairness to its author, the use of Scripture in *Pragerisches Gross und Klein* seems to us not so much a conscious presentation of sacred history *per* se as it is a literary embellishment. Extrinsic and accidental use of this kind does, of course, present a danger, and is a matter on which the late Pius XII counsels biblical interpreters, although His Holiness concedes such use within moderation for the purposes of preaching.

A literary critic may read the text and write it off as a pious and overdone use of personification, and so miss the whole point of the spiritual message Father Emmerich intended. As a means to an end, personification finds legitimate use beyond the scope of the purely artistic or literary. St. Francis de Sales, for example, that great Doctor of Devotion and French writer contemporaneous with Father Cyril, uses personification to explain union with Christ through detachment from the pleasures of self complacency. In his *Love of God* (Book VI, Chap. xi) there is a dialogue between an inquirer and a statue—the statue typifying a soul that finds itself powerless to pray. In the ensuing conversation the statue describes how its love of God involves much fundamental activity — faith, hope, charity, and humility — but the activity is such that it excludes the pleasure of achievement, even in spiritual things. The speaking statue points up the soul's confident abandonment to God, without which union with Him is never complete.

Personification employed for devotional purpose such as we find in the Emmerich stories include a sequence of cause to effect in its narration of favors received. *The more you honor Me, the more I will bless you!* Here is expressed a direct correlation, the kind and number of divine favors dependent on the kind and number of humanly good deeds performed for His glory. The requests are many and typical; the coverage of human problems alone is an appealing aspect of the early history of devotion to the divine Child-King. Significant also is the fact that each beneficiary of divine favors became in his turn an instrument in God's plan to reign on earth. All of this indicated to Father Emmerich, as it had indicated to his predecessor Father Cyril, that the Incarnate Word desires to be enthroned in human hearts. The Infant of Bethlehem is at once the King of kings, personally interested in the affairs of men.

CHAPTER 4

ENGLISH VERSION OF PRAGERISCHES GROSS UND KLEIN

(1737)

(Title Page)

The Great and Little One of Prague

Being the
Historical Deposition
Setting forth mysteries of mercy in the
miraculous happenings
of the

Great and Little

connected with His holy image made from virgin wax

Infant Jesus

Who has been worshipped for more than a hundred years at the Monastery of the Discalced Carmelites in Less Side, Prague.

By

Rev. Father Emmerich of St. Stephen, Prior of the aforementioned monks, compiled and enriched by instructive concepts from Holy Scripture, arranged in chronological order, with the Litany of the Holy Name of Jesus completing the work.

Printed at the Royal Court in Prague by Mathias Adam Hoder, Printer to the Archbishop, 1737.

(Dedication)

To

HER SERENE HIGHNESS

and

MOST EXALTED DUCHESS

Lady Maria Anna Furstenberg

nee Countess of Waldstein

Duchess of the Holy Roman Empire

When she had made waterproof a basket of reeds, the sorrowing Israelite mother laid in it her beautiful first-born male, and entrusted him to the waters of the River Nile to escape death at the hand of Pharaoh. When Pharaoh's daughter sighted the bullrush ark as she walked the river bank, she had it brought to her. The lovely baby inside she named Moses (because she drew him out of the water) and reared him with great tenderness as her own son. The child Moses grew into manhood and delivered his people, exiled from their homeland, from the bondage of their cruel Egyptian masters. Working signs and wonders in God's name he brought about the punishment of the Pharaohs who dealt thus ruthlessly with the Chosen People.

Most gracious Lady, from the very first day He appeared among us — the most merciful Infant Jesus — our heavenly Moses has been sought out for blasphemous treatment at the hands of non-believers, and no less miraculously than the child Moses has He been preserved by Divine Providence. Our Divine Moses, too, has been carried to the shores of an ungrateful world. Until the present time it would seem that the manifold wonderful graces and miraculous signs worked through the all-powerful hand of God were cast on the water of human ignorance only to be drowned in oblivion.

But today, we place His many blessings and miracles into a bullrush ark—the ark of this little book—and bring it to the sympathetic attention of Your Serene Highness, in the well-founded hope that the lovely Infant therein, received into your noble arms, will be reared and nourished by motherly love, that the princely gifts and sacrifices He has already received, confined in this narrow basket of reeds will be ever increased and His veneration ever expanded under your esteemed patronage.

Our confidence that you will do this stems from our knowledge of the renowned piety and praiseworthy zeal of your noble parents, the Count and Countess, whose honor lives on, enshrined in the twenty-two churches they built and magnificently furnished to the greater glory of God, a splendid example for the aristocracy to emulate. As further monuments to their zeal, your distinguished parents remodeled and enlarged eight other churches, seventeen deaneries, and residences for pastors and chaplains, besides sponsoring the erection of fourteen hospitals and fraternities.

Your noble father was called out of this world to his reward with the consolation of a happy death. Your mother, the Countess, has been granted the grace, through the operation of Divine Providence, to spend her last days in a convent, anticipating the enjoyment of heavenly peace. From these noble parents your Serene Highness has inherited her praiseworthy zeal to promote the honor of God at all times with a heart enkindled by an abiding love for the most gracious. Hence we are encouraged by the hope that Your Serene Highness will not only in all kindness accept our effort but will at the same time take pleasure therein.

It is quite apparent that the Little and the Great One, our merciful Infant Jesus, our divine Moses, is now crying out for pity to the princely Furstenbergs and their noble ancestors, the Counts of Waldstein. It pleases this divine Moses to manifest Himself, as the loving Bride of the Canticle relates, upon high mountains and in deep forests: *Ecce ista venit saliens in montibus! Sicut magnus inter ligna silvarum, sic dilectus meus inter filios*—like an apple tree among the woods, so is my beloved among the sons of men. (Cant. 2:3-8) Elsewhere He shines with mysterious significance as a stone in the parable of St. Paul's epistle to the Ephesians: *Ipso summo angulari lapide Christo Jesu.* (Eph. 2:20)

Therefore, we humbly request Your Serene Highness to accept this little basket wherein our merciful Infant Jesus reposes. He will Himself reward you with an abundance of heavenly blessings for increasing His honor with your maternal care.

Dutifully submitted to Your Serene Highness by the

Prior and Monks of the Monastery of
Discalced Carmelites in Prague

(Page of the approval of Religious Superior and Ecclesiastical Imprimatur)

FACULTIS ORDINIS

FR. Ildephonsus a Praesentatione B.B. Praepositus Generalis Carmelitarum Discalcestorum, Congregationis S. Eliae, Ordinis Beatissimae Virginis Mariae de Monte Carmelo, ac ejusdem S. Mentis Prior.

Dum Opusculum, cui titulus, Pragenum Magnum et Parvum, hoc est Historia Gratiosi Pueri Jesu, qui apud nostros Pragae publice colitur; a R. P.F. Emerice a S. Stephano, Provinciae nostrae S. Leopoldi in Austria Sacerdote Professo, ac Conventus nostri Pragensis Priore, Germanico. Idiomate compositum, duo ex Theologis nostris approbaverint; quantum ad nos attinet, Facultatem Impertimur, ut typis mandetur. In quorum fidem etc. Datum Panormi in Conventu nos o S. Nariae Auxiliatricis die 22 Augusti. 1737.

Fr. Ildephonsus a Praesentat. B.V.
Praepositus Generalis
Fr. Desiderius a S. Michaelo, Secretarius

CENSURA

Reverendissimi Arch-Episcopalis Officii Pragensis. Ex commissione Reverendissimi Archi-Episcopalis Officii, relationem hanc, de Amabilissimo

Jesulo revidi et ad inflammandum cora fidelium, ergo dulcissimam ejus memoriam, imprimi posse censeo. Ita tamen, ut secundum providam Authoris protestationem, non alio ea sensu quam juxta Decretum S.S. D. Urbani VIII. die 13. Martii Anno 1625. et ejusdem Declarationem 1634. die 5. Julii editam intelligentur. Dat. IN domo. Cler. Reg. S. Mariae de Provident. die 7, Septembris, Anno 1737.

D. Antonius Obiteczki, S. R. SS.
Theologiae Prof. Em. Reverendis Confistorii Assessor

IMPRIMATUR
JOANNES MAURITIUS
WENCESLAUS MARTINI,
Vicarius Generalis, & Officialis

DECLARATION

The author of this historical narrative declares that he has written solely as an historian, and hence whatever is related in this text is to be understood as a humanly credible and astonishing account (as many others have been written previously) and not as a divine miracle, sanctioned and approved by proper ecclesiastical authorities. This is hereby declared by the author duly observing the laws of the Pope.

PREFACE

You may have wondered, Child of God, why you and others who venerate images to honor and glorify God receive from His hand more graces through this particular image than others more precious and more artistic. Just what is the secret of your success in obtaining miraculous favors from the infant hand of an almighty God? St. John of the Cross has the answer in the third book, the thirty-sixth chapter of his work concerned with the Ascension of Mount Carmel. God performs more numerous miracles through this image than others, the saint reminds you, mainly because He plans to use the "little things" of this world to effect great ones and so awaken from their lethargy the souls of so-called believers, too lukewarm to rouse themselves to an abiding faith in Christ. He works the miracles, not so much for them personally of course, as for their edification through others, and a reward for the deep and unshakable faith the truly devout display through their outward veneration of this Holy Child.

John of the Cross is quite clear on the morality of the veneration of this Holy image and images in general: namely, that although the veneration is paid to a representation of a saint, the image itself is a symbol and pledge, so to speak, that the saint himself is being supplicated. For images themselves can effect no miracles. To hold that they can is contrary to the teachings of our holy faith. Replace the image for an imaginary instant with the person of Christ Himself. You call yourself a follower of

Christ, and well you may be; but would His wonderful deeds have impressed you, or would you have benefited from them at all, with faith lacking and a spirit of irreverence in your attitude to the wonder-worker, Christ? St. Luke remarks in the second chapter of his Gospel that for this very reason—the absence of believers in His divine mission, Christ worked so few miracles in His own homeland.

It is interesting and understandable why Christ worked most of His miracles elsewhere. He performed miracles, then, not so much where he was accepted and honored, but where, mingled with His friends, He found enemies who despised and defamed Him. Here was the opportunity, you see, to show the mercy and justice He had recommended for all who would be His followers. The miracles themselves are proof of His power to reward the good and punish the unjust for their incredulity.

The treatise presented here is historical proof of what has just been said concerning the miraculous power of our Lord in His role as an Infant.

You tell me that your need, spiritually speaking, is a pressing one, and one you are most anxious to confide to the Infant Jesus. You have proceeded in the proper direction; you are one of those followers of the Incarnate Son of God who see the mystery of the Triune God unfolding in the Church He founded through that Incarnate Son. It is impossible to please God without faith, the Apostle tells us. Therefore, when you come, in your need, before an image of the Son of God made man, faith in His power to help you must abide along with that need. With the great reverence that attends faith and attests it, you recognize the image for what it is: not the flesh and blood of the sacred Humanity, but His representation, connoting His Divinity, omnipotent and wise as well as merciful. Coming without reverence to His image is almost a contradiction in terms; the doubter's hopes are seldom if ever fulfilled. Faith is a prerequisite for favors from God. Faith takes precedence over other attitudes in approaching God with the prayer of petition.

Secondly, there is the attitude of supernatural hope that, through the veneration of this particular holy image, God will make good in your particular need what He promised through the mouth of the psalmist: "Because he believed in Me, I will help him; I shall protect him, for he has recognized My name. I shall be with him in his suffering, and I shall save him and show him his salvation." (Ps. 90)

The third way to approach God effectively for favors is through love, absolute love. This will require expression of your inward longing to worship the Infant Jesus as the Incarnate Son of God. This love will urge you to devote yourself to Him and pledge the performance of good works in His name among men. For the love of God you will love your neighbor who, like yourself, is the image of Him. You will be compelled, in justice, to do what Christ commanded through His apostle Matthew: "Thou shalt love the Lord thy God with all thy heart, and with all thy soul, and with all thy mind, and thou shalt love thy neighbor as thyself." (Matt. 22)

However, the way to God through faith, hope and love, as we have outlined above, is not yet terminated. There must be added that fourth factor, penance. If you come to the image of the Infant Jesus petitioning, conscious that you have offended Him personally, knowing of the sins of others, then you must be prepared to demonstrate a willingness to suffer reparation for those sins. He will expect to hear your resolve to amend, to seek spiritual improvement through confession and reception of Holy Communion. The rapport of holy friendship demands this, and divine mercy is promised upon the fulfillment of this penitential approach: Do penance, for the kingdom of heaven is at hand. (Matt. 3)

But how ought you to carry out your penitential promises? Acts of Christian justice are the natural means of reparation for sin. These include among others, a determination to worship Jesus, the Son of God, with deep humility; to carry your personal cross in recognition of His, with patience as He carried His; to resign yourself to do the will of God in your regard; to be ever aware of a neighbor who may need your charity. The archangel Raphael expressed this well when he advised Tobias: "It is good to pray and to fast and to give to the poor." Better than a treasure, the gift to the poor saves the donor from death, spiritually speaking, and sweeps away his debt of sin and obtains for him mercy and life eternal.

Father Cyril of the Mother of God, as I intend

to prove to you through an exposition of his great devotion to the Infant, was a man of great wisdom and virtue. So holy was his life and so colored with complete devotion to the cause of the Infant Jesus that it earned for him the title "Procurator of the Infant Jesus." The prayer that he composed is really a personal expression of what he himself experienced through his own practical devotion. Like others, at one time he found himself in a situation requiring immediate relief, and the words he wrote indicate how this experience widened his understanding of the needs of others:

O Infant Jesus, I take refuge in Thee
Through Thy mother's intercession
I beg Thee — save me in this hour of need . . .
For I believe, truly and sincerely,
In Thy divine power to succor me.
My faith impels me
To seek and to find mercy.
I love Thee with my heart and soul
And ruefully repent my sins.
On my knees I pray to Thee
O Infant Jesus, deliver me.
I promise to amend my ways
And never again to offend Thee.
Therefore will I sacrifice
Suffer patiently in Thy name
And serve always with fidelity.
My neighbor as myself I will love
With all my heart, and for Thy sake.
Infant Jesus, I adore Thee,
Mighty Infant, I pray Thee
Save me in this present need,
That I may enjoy Thee forever
And see Thee with Mary and Joseph.
And with the angels worship Thee. Amen.

I

INTRODUCTION

Let me open this historical treatise by posing a question about the Incarnation of the Son of God. Why, do you suppose, did the loving Christ, our merciful Savior, choose for his human entrance into this world the temporal reign of the cruel tyrant, Herod Antipas? The choice of time from all eternity was His to make: why did He not rather choose to come to earth during the earlier reign of the God-fearing David? A blood relative, a descendant of the royal house of David, Christ might have been his contemporary as well. In the history of the Hebrew race we can perceive a lesson in His choice of time, a lesson that offers much consolation.

Historians paint the period of the Jews under the reign of Herod the Great as one of great hardship for them. It was a time of persecution, with mental and physical strains, of widespread unrest and longing for a deliverer. Never, it seemed, had their need been so great. Never had they seemed farther away from a means of relief from their present affliction. Human help seemed beyond hope, when on the scene of their miserable existence appeared this Jesus, born one of their own Hebrew race, to deliver them from the slavery imposed by foreign dominantion. In the person of Jesus was the instrument of God; divine faith would bring its reward of rejuvenated hope, and a balm for their unhappy lives. The lesson for us today is obvious. Human ways and means failing, we ought never to despair, even in the hour of greatest need. Jesus is the Savior of all men, as His name signifies.

History has a way of repeating itself; and it would seem that times as hard as those of Herod for the Jews were being relived when our monastery was established in Prague in 1624. Despite the offer of His Majesty, Emperor Ferdinand II, to grant an annual income for the clergy, our priests preferred to live in poverty, supported by donations from the faithful. But soon, and unexpectedly, they found themselves deserted by their former benefactors and persecuted by the heretic enemy occupying the city of Prague. Conditions became so bad that there was not even enough bread for their daily sustenance. All they possessed was an abundance of misery—the bread of misery and the water of sufferings that David mourned in his desolation: "Tears were my food, night and day."

At a time when they would seem to have reached the depths of human misery, and feeling all but deserted by God and man, they experienced a sudden and unsolicited relief from Princess Polyxena of Lobkowitz. The Father of Mercy had not, after all, deserted his followers. This noble-woman sent them an image of the Incarnate Son, the waxen form of the dear Infant Jesus, whose miraculous history we intend to relate. The Father of Mercies took this manner of answering the pleas of his desperately tried and suffering priests: Come and worship here, dear sons, the merciful Infant Jesus represented in this holy image. In Him you will have a solicitous foster father, a mighty protector and an ever faithful helper in future need.

II

FIRST FAVORS FROM THE HOLY IMAGE

The waters of the pond Siloe are reputed for their healing power. Yet for most of those who, creeping in their infirmity, came each year to its edges, only one might expect to walk away cured. Compared with Siloe, Jesus, our fount of healing, is a veritable river, flowing with unending mercies. In the history of the Holy Image, you will discover not the measured depth of Siloe, but the unending river of mercy that is the wondrous love of Jesus. Here the blind receive sight, the deaf their hearing, the mute are made to speak, the sick regain health, the half-dead return to life, and those in need find saving help.

The Fathers of the monastery displayed the beautiful image in their oratory and places of worship, and took their turns praying before it daily for two hours. The Prior recommended this devotional practice, realizing that through it his monks would learn true humility. It fitted in perfectly with the primary purpose of the priestly vocation, namely worship of God, in this case, the Divine Infant. Such a call to humility, in one sense, can never be restricted to the priesthood. It is a call to which all men are invited: "Learn of Me, for I am meek and humble of heart." The innocent of heart partake of the privileges of children; these above others have the power to move the heart of God to grant them favors.

The year 1628 began to unfold itself in our history as a year of extraordinary favors. For some reason, the heart of Ferdinand was disposed once again to offer monetary help to his Carmelites in Prague. Once before they had refused the royal offer; now they recognized in him an instrument of aid in their stricken condition, and accredited the Holy Infant with providing the royal benefactor. By imperial decree, the Bohemian Council was directed to send them supplies monthly from the royal farms, and to provide a two-thousand florin payment for the ordinary maintenance of the monastery. This first grace from the Infant came unexpectedly, and was an indication that in the future they might expect a continuance of His fatherly care. In this they were not disappointed. Proof of it lay in the state of the vineyards included in the monastic lands. These lands had lain fallow for want of funds for cultivation. But around 1630, they began to yield unbelievable harvests. Here literally was the application of our Lord's words to His disciples: "I am the True Vine, and My Father is the Keeper of the Vine; you are the branches. Without Me you are powerless. If you keep faith with Me, and My words stay with you, you may ask for anything you want, and you will receive it. But, if you leave Me (withhold your love and devotion) you shall be cast away like a branch that has withered."

The two graces I have mentioned are common

to priests and others who embrace the monastic life. What I shall speak about now is a special favor granted by the Infant Jesus upon one among us, who had suffered a veritable purgatory of dryness of spirit. The pleasure his brother novices derived from devotion to the Infant Jesus inspired him with courage to ask for relief from this affliction of spirit. This occurred during the celebration of Christmas in the year 1629. The holy season found him praying fervently and with humility to be relieved of his darkness of mind. The true path to the perfection of priesthood was something he continually petitioned; he begged that his eyes might search for and recognize this path, and that his heart might be encouraged to embrace the duties, which fulfilled, would merit his eternal happiness.

Consider the intense happiness of this monk, therefore, when in one ecstatic moment during a rapturous meditation he felt a wonderful light of love illumine him. It enveloped his soul completely. In the midst of the flame of this intense love, there came a calm and peace that he had not experienced for more than thirty years. He was, so to speak, reborn. Spiritually deaf and dumb during so long a time away from God, he now was able to discern the things of the spirit and to praise God. Formerly unable to make proper judgments on the morality of things, now his vision cleared, and he embraced the good with as much ardor as he abhorred the evil. Prayer itself had been a burden to his soul; without a spoken word, he could now commune with God. In a word, the path to perfection seemed no longer blocked to him. Eternal happiness lay with the fulfillment of his monastic profession, and the challenge to attain that perfect aim in life filled him with a holy desire.

III

THE MIRACULOUS IMAGE FALLS INTO THE HANDS OF UNBELIEVERS

During a battle with Amalec, Moses, the leader of the Israelites and the Lord's close friend, made his way up the mountain, there to implore the help of Jahweh for a victory of his people over their enemy. Holy Scripture records the fact that so long as Moses upheld his hands in supplication to God, that long were the Israelites victorious. Amalec gained ground, so it seemed, only when Moses relaxed that gesture of uplifted hands, dangerously threatening the Israelites with defeat. A similar relationship existed between the monks and their divine Infant. A steady stream of prayer directed to that Holy Image won them an uninterrupted flow of grace. At such times they were blessed with royal benefactions. But when in 1630 the novitiate was transferred from Prague to Munich, there was a break in this stream of devotions and prayers from the devotees of the Infant, and gradually the whole monastery felt a certain withdrawal of divine benediction. It was a time of great need, almost to the point of impoverishment. No doubt it was all a part of the plan of Providence. For without great impetus to drive them to seek refuge in the power of the Infant Jesus, they might have continued unaffected in their daily living, and in this way unknowingly deprived the Divine Child of the opportunity, humanly speaking, of showing them His favors.

The previous chapter of this treatise dealt with the benevolent mercy of God. What must be related here and now are instances, equally impressive of the justice and punishment of God.

When in 1631, for example, the city of Prague was in state of siege by its Saxon enemies, Father Cyril and his fellow priests fled the monastery. In the emergency, none of them remembered to bring away the miraculous image, which was left behind in a chapel soon to be sacked by heretic "Praedicantes." Conquest of the city was quickly followed by desecration of its churches. The monastery church became the scene of heretical service, and the two priests who had remained behind were imprisoned under guard of fifteen soldiers. What happened to the holy image as a result is painful to relate. In hateful sport the invaders treated it so roughly that both hands were broken, after which they cast it aside. In view of the miracles it would later effect in the lives of others, the present miracle was that such rough treatment would leave the image at all intact, escaping only with damaged members. Strangely enough, for all the disreputable manner of its handling, the image itself remained unsoiled, notwithstanding the fact that it lay unprotected and abused during seven years of neglect. The monastery, all this time, was indisputable proof of the words of St. Thomas Aquinas: *Sic nos tu visitas, sicut te colimus.* (In the way in which we worship You, in such a way will You redeem us.)

But a day of victory finally arrived. Imperial troops marched into Prague on May 25, 1632, and the Prior and his Carmelites were able to return from exile and take up residence again in their monastic home. Perhaps in the flush of victory and the business of resettling affairs to normal living, there lies some explanation of why the devotion to the Infant suffered neglect on the part of His former devotees. The realization of this fact stood out and took on painful significance with the issuance of a royal decree the next year by Ferdinand III, now successor to his father and the new King of Bohemia. The annuity which his father, Ferdinand II had granted to the monks he now decreed henceforth terminated. Taxes on the monastic vineyards soon became too burdensome for payment. By legal process the monks were now deprived even of the use and care of their lands. It was an old story painfully re-enacted: poverty became penury, and their misery was acute to the point of becoming unbearable.

With the rumor that the Swedish leader, General Panyr (Banner) was laying down a strategy to attack and besiege the city, the situation was aggravated for everyone concerned. For Father Felician of St. Bartholomew, the prior of Carmel and his priests, it meant a hasty decision to evacuate and move back to Munich, which only a few months previously, they had left in favor of Prague, as a center of novitiate training. It was a temporary measure, fortunately, lasting only until the enemy was routed from Prague. The brief aftermath of war this time included an outbreak of the plague, to which Father Felician himself fell victim and died after a brief illness on October 28, 1634.

A summary of the disorders and temporal misery that befell the monastery at this time would be incomplete without mention of the case of a novice whose conduct had some bearing on the Holy Image of the Infant Jesus. Entrusted with the duties of sacristan, he failed to measure up to the trust; in fact he greatly disappointed his superiors, who had given him this responsibility because he had up to this time shown such aptitude for the care of the house of God, and for the promise he displayed of becoming the model religious in all things.

It will be remembered that the monastery, recently liberated from invaders, bore signs of their irreverent occupancy. The state of the chapel was deplorable. It was while searching curiously through the debris stacked hastily behind the altar, that the novice-sacristan in our case history, came finally upon the statue of the Infant King which we mentioned before as once being the pride and joy of the monks. Whether through malice or childish indifference on his part it is difficult to say, but the unexpected thing happened. Though uncovered and recognized, the image was left in a pitiable condition, an act committed in haste, perhaps, but not with impunity. The young monk, heretofore remarkable for his exact obedience and humble submission to his superiors, displayed qualities painfully the opposite. And this changed attitude became so marked and scandalous that he gained the unenviable reputation of being possessed by a devil. Never at rest with himself or with others, he was finally dismissed from the novitiate.

All unknown to the rest of the monks, the miraculous image lay hidden and neglected. There continued to be a noticeable restlessness on the part of all the monks, something undefinable, that blocked their path to peace. It infected the atmosphere; it affected personalities, among the ranks and among those in command. The records of the monastery confirm the fact that no prior, sub-prior, or novice-master could last longer than three years through this period of hardship and trouble. One priest after the other asked to be transferred to another house of the Order. This state of affairs naturally alarmed the provincial superiors. They were completely unaware of the reason for this widespread discontent. We understand, as they did not, that the misery was plainly the expression of the absence of Divine blessing upon the house.

IV
OUT OF THE DARKNESS INTO THE LIGHT

You will recall that hardly had the birth of Our Blessed Lord been accomplished, and the Incarnation a recorded fact of history, than Herod set into motion a plot to destroy His young life. Upon divine orders, the Babe fled in the arms of His mother and St. Joseph to the temporary freedom of Egypt. Hidden as it were under the veil of dark paganism, he remained there until divinely ordered again He was called back to the lightness of the land of Israel. As His prophet Osee expresses the event of His banishment and return: *"Ex Aegypto vocavi filium meum."* (I have called My Son out of Egypt.)

There is an analogy here with the experience of the waxen image of that Infant, honored briefly in Prague, then suddenly robbed of His veneration by heretic hands and driven into the Egypt of a dark and unwholesome place, behind the very altar where He had formerly been venerated. But just as the biblical sojourn came to its end in God's good time, so passed the seven years of neglect, ending in 1637.

With the opening of the Pentecost season, one of the novices was recalled by his superiors to Prague from Munich. He was one of the group who remained faithful in venerating the Infant Jesus. His own historical treatment of the holy image of Prague reveals that he is the monk already mentioned who, after years of desolation and spiritual darkness, received the light of divine consolation through petitioning the Infant Jesus. From his testimony we learn what occurred not many months after his coming to Prague, when enemy Swedish troops marched into the city intent on taking it by force. Bohemia, of course, stood to suffer in many ways if their plans would carry. With its downfall would come also a calamitous blow to the Catholic faith, recently restored in Prague. To avert the imminent danger, Father Prior gave orders to his monks to petition Heaven with great fervor of soul for the wrath of God to be withheld from the unfortunate city. Here was the opportunity Cyril had been waiting for. Now he could press his intention to search for the lost treasure he knew could bring success to their campaign of prayer. The search proved fruitful; he lost no time in removing the image from its dusty debris and with permission set it up in the common, or community room of the monastery for all to venerate. It is not difficult to conjure up the joy with which Cyril urged his fellow monks to join in rejoicing at the newly found treasure. It was a common sight to find him kneeling in rapturous devotion in front of the image. His fellow religious were prepared, then, to hear him report words which the Infant spoke on one such occasion: "Have mercy on Me and I shall have mercy on you. Give Me My hands, that I can give you peace. As you worship Me, so will I heed your prayers."

Pondering the words he had heard, Father Cyril was moved to searching thought: was the mournful tone the Infant had used an indication that He desired reparation for the irreverence and indifference He was suffering? Was the present state of affairs in the monastery with its poverty, its restless spirit and lack of security, the just punishment for the treatment the holy image had received, not only from heretic enemies, but also from his friends and former devotees as well? These thoughts constrained him to remain in choir longer than his fellow monks after their common devotion. Alone, he approached the statue and removed the blue cover that served as a robe, and found the painful truth. The hands were indeed in a pitiful state of disfigurement: the Infant had good cause to complain. Filled with compassion, Father Cyril realized his responsibility to make this matter known. Aloud he promised to sacrifice, cost what it might, to make immediate efforts to restore His little hands to Christ. In the light of what happened subsequently, Father Cyril's resolve that day must have pleased the little Infant immensely. For as events turned out, devotion among the Carmelites of Prague was very soon restored, and the image, renovated, became once again an object of their community veneration. Many blessings stemmed from this renewal of fervor —not the least of which was the military turn of the tide that wiped out the invader from the city of Prague, and provided the monastery with temporal means to live in peace.

V

MIRACLES AFTER THE RESTORATION OF HANDS

Father Cyril of the Mother of God frequently quoted *Ecclesiastes* on how it displeased the Lord God for men not to fulfill their promises and resolutions or to postpone them: "When you vowest a vow, defer not to pay it for He hath no pleasure in fools. It is better not to vow than to vow and not pay it."

It was not likely that Father Cyril would forget the promise He made to the Infant to have the hands of the holy image restored. For this reason he took the statue to his superior for permission and aid to carry out his plan. He explained the message of the Infant, and in enthusiasm to enlist his help, he reminded Father Prior, in the words of St. John, that nothing given in the name of God goes without its reward. "Give and thou shalt be given." But the Prior, reminding Cyril of the many important temporal needs of the monastery, would not commit himself to defray the expense which rehabilitation of the image would incur.

Saddened at the refusal, but not completely disheartened, Father gathered the image into his arms and returned it to a table in his cell in the monastery. On his knees in front of the statue, he begged the Infant to move his superior to a change of heart. He prayed the Blessed Mother to use her maternal influence for the honor of her divine Child to move the mind of some benefactor to donate something of his worldly goods that would make possible the spending of money for this pious purpose. How this fervent prayer was answered within three days is told by Father Cyril himself, when he afterwards recalled in writing certain events which have been the original source of much of this history of the Great and Little One of Prague:

Within three days' time of this ardent prayer of Cyril, God in His merciful providence sent a venerable old man, pious and well-known in his native city of Assig, by name Benedictus Manskonig. On a visit to Prague in 1637, he was stricken with serious illness. There appeared no hope for his recovery. The call for the ministrations of the last rites came to the monastery, and Father Cyril was sent to his bedside. He heard the old man's confession and prepared him for his journey to eternity. Conscious, however, and disposed to hear the monk's story, he listened to Father Cyril talk with great fervor on the power of the Holy Infant to work miracles. The story of the disfigured hands of the image touched the dying man to offer, then and there, a hundred florins for the restoration of its hands.

It would be perfectly reasonable to suppose that a pious, intelligent man like the Prior would find it agreeable to give Father Cyril an unqualified affirmative as answer to his fervent request; he, in his position of authority, would certainly understand that without help, the monk would find it difficult if not impossible to discharge his obligation to the Infant. But Divine Providence, apparently, willed the answer to be negative. The Prior explained quite patiently that the monastery in its present state of economy had other more urgent needs. What he did do, surprisingly soon, was to order a new and beautiful image of the Infant, at greater cost than it would have been to renovate the broken one. The incident had at least this happy feature—that it tested Father Cyril's obedience and gave him opportunity to deny his own will in the matter.

But the Infant Jesus provided an astonishing way

in which to make clear His own will in this matter: the new statue, placed upon the altar for the first time, was dislodged by a falling candelabra, and was broken beyond any hope of repair. The lesson seemed quite clear. The Infant had asked for the original image to be mended. This was the image through which He had received veneration, and had suffered neglect; this was the image in which He wanted now to receive homage and reparation. Father Prior, however, was not convinced of this truth; and for his stubborness in the matter, he suffered. "As you will honor Me, I will do unto you," had been the Infant's promise. His monks noted the change in his attitude and manner; they found him difficult, almost unbearable in his relations with them. And he himself became so depressed and dissatisfied that it was a happy release for the monastery when he was relieved by appeal to higher authority of his responsibility as prior.

The provincial appointments of 1638 brought a new Prior to the charge of the monastery in Prague. It was years now since Father Cyril had made his first request for the mending of the statue and at the first opportunity he laid his problem before the newly installed superior. The Prior listened kindly and interestedly to the suggestion that such a permission granted would be guarantee of God's blessing on him and his new office. He agreed that the Infant had indeed secured favors for the monastery in its previous need, but the answer was a tempered refusal. He pointed as his predecessor had done to the gravely acute financial distress still prevailing in the Carmel of Prague. Perhaps, he suggested, it would be quite in order if the Infant would work a miracle by filling the depleted coffers of the monastery! After these doubtful words of comfort, Cyril betook himself again to the privacy of his cell, and alone with the damaged image, prayed for the material and temporal needs of his Order. If these were relieved, he reasoned, there would be little excuse left for a negative answer to his request.

He had scarcely finished his fervent petition, addressed through the Blessed Virgin, when a call of duty took him into the church. There he was met by a stranger of aristocratic bearing, who advanced toward him bearing a gift in her hand. She smiled, then disappeared, after addressing Father Cyril with these words: "This gift God in His Providence has sent to relieve your poverty."

The donation was more than enough to take care both of the present needs and the restoration of the damaged hands, a task which the Prior acting immediately gave into Cyril's personal care. His first expression of grateful delight was to kneel before the image, and in great simplicity and joy, thank him for this favor. There was, however, one stipulation the Prior had insisted on, and so instructed the lay brother charged with taking the statue from the monastery to have it repaired. The cost was not to exceed one gulden; arrangements were not to be made for work costing more than this amount. Once again, Father Cyril met with disappointment! The Infant would have to wait, it seemed, until some beneficent person should come to the monastery, led there for the sole purpose of mending the little hands of the Infant Christ! And come he did, as the records show.

VI

A LONGED-FOR BENEFACTOR IS FOUND AT LAST

It is a quality of truly human love, and a very natural one, to reach out a helping hand to those in need of sympathy. One may claim himself a Christian and by baptism therefore a child of God, possessed also of many Christian virtues, but unless he exhibits this virtue of fraternal love, he is not entirely human. Even Christ, the divine man, the God made man through the Incarnation, would lack human appeal without this characteristic human trait, without His deeply sympathetic heart and a love that kept him moving, restless, forever doing good among men. Like his model, Father Cyril of the Mother of God was motivated by a deep and abiding love for others. He loved the Infant Jesus, represented by this little image, with all his human heart; and the continued loss of the hands of his dear "Infant" cost him real suffering. Never a day passed that he did not pray with tears of petition for the means to repair that loss.

In such a prayerful state one day, he heard distinctly a voice within him say: "Place Me at the entrance of the sacristy and you will find someone there who will take pity on Me." Obediently the pious priest carried the image of the Infant to the designated place. The act was one of blind obedience, and returning to his cell Cyril could only make an act of hope that he had not been deceived. As certainly as the Infant had promised, his prayer was answered. A visitor to the church stopped out of curiosity at the door of the sacristy. He caught sight of the image placed there under obedience and moved with pity for its damaged condition, he mentioned the matter to the Prior, to whom he had come on business. Generously he offered to have the statue mended at his personal expense, an offer which the Prior promptly accepted, to Father Cyril's deep satisfaction. The restored hands, carved in wood and covered with wax, added beauty to the little image that Cyril carried, in grateful joy, back to the church for veneration.

It is never God's way to be outdone in generosity. His manner of acting with men is rather to return good for good a hundredfold. The truth of this observation is proved by subsequent events in the life of this benefactor.

When this good man later met with financial reverses that brought him to the verge of losing his reputation among his creditors, he was suddenly spared the trouble and embarrassment that seemed unavoidable by receiving unexpected good news. Formerly employed by the government, he had never received complete remuneration for years of service, and entertained no prospect of being paid his lapsed salary. Just as his own personal loan was coming due, he received a notification that he would be reimbursed for his work, a circumstance he attributed to devotion to the Infant. Furthermore this pious man was experiencing marital unhappiness caused by the naturally unlovable character of his wife. There had been serious breaches of domestic peace, and conditions seemed to warrant a separation. The conflict had reached a point where threats had been made, and a spirit of mutual unforgiveness had discouraged any attempt at reconciliation. But with the husband's dedication to the Infant, and his attention to the material needs of the image, there was granted him a spirit of resignation to the will of God. With a changed heart he invited his estranged wife to return home, where they lived together in peace and joy. One incident in their later life deserves mention here. The husband and wife, no longer poor, owned a treasure box, where they kept money and valuables. This customarily was locked and laid away securely every night without too much thought about the possibility of being robbed. One night, however, petty thieves broke in and were about to carry the box off as their loot, when an unexplained commotion frightened off the thieves. Thus one can apply to this benefactor of the Infant the words of St. John in his first epistle: "Have you not surrounded his house and all his belongings by a wall? You have blessed the work of his hands and his wealth has increased on earth."

VII

A JUST JUDGMENT IS REAPED BY FATHER PRIOR

Writing of the Son of the Most High, Moses describes Him as carrying a fiery law in his right hand. *"In dextera ejus ignes lex."* (Deut. 33:2) Solomon's description points to the wealth and glory that the Most High carries in His left hand: *"In sinistra ejus divitiae et gloria."* (Prov. 3). We can see this description verified in the case of our beloved Infant Jesus, the true Son of God. To those who worship Him the Lord showed mercy, wealth and glory, and gracious benevolence, the gifts of His left hand. Against those who neglect to promote His honor or overlook it, He showed raised a right hand with its penalty of fire and revenge. Proof of this we shall set forth in the following incident.

For his long neglect of the statue, the prior whose aid Father Cyril had tried to enlist came in time to reap a just judgment. The occupation troops on one maurading trip visited the monastery and secretly made off with six work horses. They followed this theft by leading off some of the cattle from the monastery fields. The cattle loss meant reduced dairy products for the monks' maintenance. The horses used for hauling quarry loads were an important factor in their building program. The combined loss meant that the economy of the Carmel would suffer. And this was the case. Voluntary donations were not forthcoming, sufficient to maintain the monks in Prague. In this emergency Father Prior sent some of his priests to other monasteries. To certain ones he assigned the task of begging. These monks, exposed to the epidemic of plague then raging, fell victims themselves or upon their return home, spread the infection to those who had not ventured outside the monastery. The situation was made all the worse by the fact that the minor officers of the monastery contracted the disease: in their turn the cook, the collector, and the tailor fell ill. Hardly one of the priests escaped without sharing some part of the misery that was the common lot of the inhabitants of Prague during the epidemic. Father Prior himself suffered most. Medical means were tried in vain to restore him to health. It seemed as if the Order would surely lose this efficient administrator, this man of great virtue and wisdom. The monks hesitated to suggest a last port of refuge, remembering that the sick man was the very person who had previously neglected to advance the cause of the Little King of Prague. But Father Prior himself consented to join them in begging a miracle from the Infant. And the case turned out to be one where the "hand of the Lord had struck, and His hand brought healing." With a childlike confidence he now placed his life in the little hands he had so reluctantly permitted to be restored. At death's door he vowed that if he were spared, he would celebrate Mass before the holy image nine consecutive times, and become henceforth and for the remainder of his life a zealous propagator of the devotion.

Within the next few days a complete return to

health was effected. The Prior lost no time fulfilling his promise, and not the least part of his change of heart was to provide a new place, more worthy than the niche it occupied in the oratory, for public veneration of the image of the Little One of Prague.

VIII

MIRACLES WORTHY OF NOTE

Signs of special favors and miracles worked for those who believed were plentiful enough to attract favorable attention to the Infant of Prague. And there had been cases of punishment for neglect and non-belief that ordinarily should have been proof for those who asked a sign. "If you see not signs and wonders, you do not believe," the little Infant might have reproached the many persons who withheld their complete allegiance. Certainly the monks were eye-witnesses of special graces. They had seen the healing of their Prior against all medical odds. But they were the exceptions rather than the rule of the times. Something else was needed to convince the outside world of its need to venerate the Infant King.

It was the Carmelite sacristan who urged public veneration, and who took his own method of securing it. Every feast day it was his zealous custom to "borrow" the image from its niche in the oratory and exhibit it in the church. On one such mission, his eagerness to transport the statue safely met with ill success. He stumbled nervously on steps leading from the monastic enclosure into the area of the church. He tripped and fell, with the shocking result that the image was once more damaged. There was much lamenting over the accident, the monk accusing himself of carelessness and with a mind to report the matter immediately to his superior.

Before there was time to do so, however, a mentally unbalanced parishioner, appearing from nowhere, so it seemed, threw himself at the stunned sacristan. Frenzied and in the act of choking the monk, the man was finally beaten off by Father Cyril who came running to his rescue. Though he had saved the sacristan and also the image from violent hands, Father Cyril was again grieved over the new development. He could find neither rest nor peace of mind until he poured out prayers of petition before the holy image, begging for some means to undo the present damage. Once more God in His providence provided, in the person of Daniel Wolff de Argentorato, retired Colonel and War Commissar of the Royal Army. The sight of the image he had previously cared for and become devoted to, deeply moved this benefactor, who lost no time in having its former beauty restored. And how highly this benefaction pleased the Infant, one can judge from the reward which came in time to Colonel Wolff.

Colonel Wolff was seized by a severe illness that puzzled his physicians and became in time hopeless. Everyone else gave up hope for his recovery, but the sick man himself. Unshaken in faith that the Infant would hear his prayers for recovery, he added a promise to his petitions: spared from death he would provide a fitting sanctuary for veneration of the image. In a few days he began to mend in health, to the amazement of all concerned. The tabernacle was set up, as he had promised, and along with this gift he paid his grateful thanks to his divine physician, the Infant Jesus, with a crucifix of ivory upon silver, two brass candelabras, a supply of candles and flower vases for decoration of the shrine. It will be the theme of the following chapter to relate certain miracles that occurred during the construction of this first real shrine of the image of Prague.

IX

BLASPHEMERS MEET WITH INSTANT PUNISHMENT

Do you remember that the crime of Oza made him subject to punishment by sudden death, a proof of divine justice? *"Mortuus est ibi justa arcam Dei."* (He met death next to the ark of God.) Holy Scripture reveals the story: When the cart upon which rested the arc was in danger of turning over, after two oxen driving the cart stumbled, Oza, afraid that the precious arks might tumble to the ground, reached out his hand to secure them. It was a bold act, one that the Lord punished immediately. Oza was struck dead beside the Ark of the Lord. (2 Kings 6:3) If the "indignation of the Lord was enkindled against Oza" because he boldly reached out a hand, how much reason must the Lord have to be angry with those who boldly open their mouth to slander and abuse the holy image of the living God?

The benefactor whose remarkable cure was related in the last chapter hastened to carry out his promise without delay. The new tabernacle he designed would require the services of a locksmith and a carpenter. These he engaged to begin the work immediately, without regard to cost. The workmen delivered the tabernacle at the appointed time arranged, but their service charge was outrageously high for the amount of work it represented, although they were paid nevertheless. The money they spent on drinking at a nearby tavern, and in their drunken state were heard to publicly ridicule and mock the Infant, calling it an idol. Both of them apostates from the Catholic faith, this was their last infamous act, for they soon contracted the plague and died miserable deaths. God is a just judge, and men must pay for their sins of slander either in this world or the next.

X

THE CURE OF THE DEAF-MUTE

It is related in the life of our Savior upon earth, that a woman cured of an illness sang out in praise of Him: *"bene omnia fecit, et muros fecit loqui et surdos audire."* (He did all things well. He made the deaf to hear and the dumb to speak.) Such a song of praise could well have come from the lips of Elizabeth Kolowrat, wife of Henry Liebsteisky, Baron von Kolowrat, high steward of the imperial Kingdom of Bohemia.

The time was July, 1639, and for some time the Baroness had suffered a grievous illness that left her without voice or hearing. The best of physicians had been consulted. Their opinions concurred that she would not live long. Much depressed at this news, her husband turned with confidence to the divine Infant of Prague, who, he heard, radiated the power of healing, *(quia virtus de illo exibat)* and made a promise on condition of his wife's recovery. Then he proceeded to ask Father Cyril to bring the image of the Infant into the presence of his sick wife. At first the priest hesitated to comply with this unusual request, but moved by the urgency of the matter, he consented. The patient was of course unable to speak, but Father Cyril held the little image to her lips for a moment. The Countess fingered its robes with reverence, and opening her eyes for the first time in hours, pressed a kiss upon the face of the divine Infant. Regaining complete consciousness almost at once, the sick woman recovered and demonstrated to all around that she could both hear and speak. In gratitude for this miracle she vowed the gift of a gold crown for her benefactor, the Infant King.

Nor did the Count, her husband, forget his part in the promise. During the remainder of his life his donations to Carmel were generous and frequent. Furthermore, he arranged an annuity in

Mass stipends to the amount of three thousand florins for masses in his memory.

This was not the only miracle performed at the royal household of Lobkowitz and Kolowrat. Some months later the Countess arranged a trip to the family country estate. All plans were in readiness, and she sat in the company of her husband in their carriage at the entrance to their home prepared to depart. The driver was given the signal to leave. Sweating, his horses kept struggling to obey his direction, but in vain. The vehicle remained rooted to the spot, notwithstanding the combined six-horse-powered efforts. There seemed to be no explanation, until the Countess remembered she had left behind the little image which had brought about her cure. Its proper place, by this time, was in the monastery, for others to venerate, not in the house she was ready to vacate. Father Cyril was sent for and the image returned to its familiar niche in the Carmel of Prague.

XI

THE SCANDAL OF THE STOLEN IMAGE

During the siege of the city of Jericho, Joshua, who directed the attack, ordered his soldiers not to plunder the city for its gold and silver. All of it was sacred, and was to be disposed for the care of the Lord. But Achan, it will be remembered, disobeyed the orders of his commander, and pillaged for his own purposes, stealing precious metals for himself. The entire army suffered for this blasphemous act, and the Lord was not pleased until satisfaction was rendered. This was accomplished by the people themselves, who took up stones and hurled them, stoning the culprit to his death.

There is a parallel to be sought in the case of one who dares to remove from its place of honor the sacred image of the divine Son of God.

The incident we have brought to your consideration took place in December of 1639 on the anniversary of the birth of our Savior. The Infant King, dressed in robes of splendor, excited the mind of a woman visitor to the church to attempt to steal the image from its shrine. A person of noble birth, she was attended by two maid servants. She ordered them to remove the statue from its niche, leaving behind the jewelry and the crown recently placed on its head. Scarcely had the three reached home with the stolen treasure, when Father Cyril as if inspired, was drawn to enter the Church. As usual his first glance was toward the shrine of the Infant. Imagine if you can his sense of loss at seeing the empty niche! *Quaesivi quem deligit anima mea, et non inveni* (I have searched for the One Whom my soul loves; I have searched for Him and have not found Him), he might have said with the psalmist. Grieved but hopeful he turned to the Infant's holy Mother and His faithful foster-father, Joseph, petitioning them to restore their lost child. "Grieve not," he heard the comforting words, "Grieve not; the lost will be found and the crime punished."

Such was the providence of God that not long afterwards a sick call brought Father Cyril to the very house where the Infant had been taken after its confiscation. The patient, one of the maids who had collaborated in the theft, confessed her deed to the priest. Her mistress did likewise, but both of them withheld their consent to restitution unless an image similar to that stolen had been promised them. Father Cyril indulgently permitted this condition, and after reprimanding the culprits, returned home with the beloved Infant.

But like the Philistines of old, these evil-doers were not permitted to go unpunished in the sight of God. These pagans, you will remember, dared to search the inner recesses of the stolen ark of the covenant, and placed its contents before their pagan idol, Bagen. For such blasphemous conduct they were meted out miserable deaths, one after the other, until the ark was returned to the Israelites.

Something of a similar nature took place in the home of the thieves. The stolen image was anything but a source of comfort; rather its very presence was a reproach, condemning their conduct. They had no peace until it was returned, and the penalty exacted was the death of one of the maid servants; the other girl, remorseful and penitent, was spared after her full confession and promise of amendment for her scandalous act. As for their mistress, the perpetrator of the deed, like Achan, she was seized with a sudden excruciating pain of body that intensified the torture of the soul. For months she lay bedridden, gout taking its steady and painful toll of her hands and feet. She lived to relate the story of her conversion, but before her gradual return to health, she was afflicted with distress of mind through her son. His marriage with one of her servants caused the family disgrace and created something of a scandal among their aristocratic circle. As if collectively this were not enough punishment, she was made to suffer still another: occupation troops in the city looted her family estate, and made off with its treasures, setting fire behind them. Thereafter she was forced to live in poverty and disgrace, abandoned by friends who were influenced by worldly considerations, among them the memory of her son's unfortunate marriage.

XII

WITHOUT FLOWERS THE INFANT WAS NOT PLEASED

The bride in the Canticle sings: *Dilectus meus mihi, et ego illi:* My beloved belongs to me and I to Him; I love Him and He loves me. I belong to Him completely and He belongs to me completely. Could one ask more of a soul, that it may please the Lord? *Qui pascitur inter lilia:* Who pastured among the lilies? My spouse takes pleasure and joy among the lilies and the well-scented flowers, therefore the bride cries out, pleading: *Fulcite me flori-*

bus. Make me strong with flowers; without them I cannot please my loved one.

This mystical song of the Canticle was well known to the procurator of the Infant Jesus. His own love for the Infant Jesus was always intense, yet it seemed to him always insufficient. True, he had searched diligently for the stolen image; he had recovered it from the home of miscreants, as we have related in the foregoing chapter. Yet Cyril of the Mother of God yearned for more certitude of his graces with the Infant. He found himself pondering further ways to express his personal love, and to repair the wrong committed against his little King. Hence it occurred to him that flowers might be the proper expression of his devotion. And this desire to venerate the image as "One who pastures among the lilies" led him one day to beg a floral gift from the sacristan. But because the latter was unwilling to part with those he had planned as a decoration for the main altar, fearing perhaps to run himself short of the customary bouquets, the sacristan denied him this favor. That such lack of generosity displeased the Infant was soon evident. The otherwise pious and devoted sacristan was tortured with discontent, and overwhelmed with sadness of soul. Fortunately he searched his soul for the reason for this change, and was given the light to recognize that what pain he now experienced was but a just penalty for his ungenerous deed. Repentant, he asked forgiveness of the Infant. As a peace offering he brought before His shrine a vase of flowers extraordinarily beautiful, and pledged himself to spread the veneration of the divine Child wherever and whenever opportunity presented itself. Those associated with the sacristan-monk noticed almost immediately his changed attitude. Depression of spirit lifted to restore him to light and peace and his former cheerfulness.

XIII

THE MONASTERY IS AGAIN DELIVERED FROM GREAT DISTRESS

Scitote, quia nullus speravit in Domino et confusus est. Know you that no one was hurt who trusted in God. In these words the wise man of God excites us to greater trust by testifying to God's unfailing kindness to men. Lessons in confidence in God are often gained by first-hand testimony, as the experience we are about to relate will prove.

The Prior of the Carmel in Prague had witnessed personally certain miracles brought about through the power of the Infant. He himself, you recall, was brought back to health when humanly speaking he was on the verge of dying. He had not forgotten this benefaction. More often than ever before he arranged to celebrate his daily Mass before the shrine of the Infant. More frequently than others, he was seen kneeling in prayer in the chapel, giving good example to his community. So implicitly did he trust the divine Child that nothing seemed impossible for him to bring to his prayers of petition. Like

David, the royal prophet, the Prior could lament: *Pauper sum ego.* Poverty in this biblical sense, of course, means a lack of moral strength. Remembering his former attitude toward the Infant's restoration, Father Prior saw in the prophet's lament a parallel to his own case.

The Prior had good reason to confess his poverty. Because he knew himself to be partly responsible for that poverty, his sentiments of humility in the face of it were sincere and profound. His was a just punishment from God. He and his monks, those whom he had not sent off to other monasteries, had barely enough for their daily sustenance. The sight of their daily misery inflicted new wounds of responsibility. With a heavily burdened heart, the Prior brought his affliction over this state of affairs to the Comforter of all afflicted, the Giver of all daily bread—the Infant Jesus. Each evening he gathered his monastic family for devotions in the chapel, expressly petitioning the Infant to aid His afflicted servants. Within three days there came a direct answer to these ardent prayers: the monastery larder was filled to its capacity; along with food in abundance there came a supply of other temporal necessities. Great was the rejoicing over the goodness of God to his children. Wisely had the words of a prophet been fulfilled in their regard: *Nullus speravit in Domino et confusus est.* Truly no one who has placed his hope in God was ever put to shame. *Desiderium pauperum exaudivit Dominus.* Indeed, the Lord had heard the longing of his poor.

XIV

A PRIEST IS SAVED FROM SPIRITUAL RUIN

Even among the chosen band of Apostles, there was one avaricious, disloyal and evil member. Have I not chosen twelve, and one of you is a devil? Christ said this, pointing to a defection among the twelve he had called as council. No one ought be scandalized, therefore, to find one monk among others who likewise defaults, who is even more than non-observant. Even the evil-minded restless monk can be found among the good and the holy. The Order itself should not suffer any shame or feel a stigma because of the infidelity of an individual. For in such a case one ought to remember the words of St. Paul: *"Oportet et haereses esse, ut et qui probati sunt, manifesti iant in vobis":* There must be heresies in order to expose those who conduct themselves as such among you.

A certain Carmelite monk (whose name we prefer to withhold) was transferred to Prague by order of his superior, and assigned there to a task that proved very disagreeable. While in this situation he was severely tempted against his vocation. The temptation grew, and there followed discouragement and the desire to renounce his monastic life. Before he could remove his holy habit and return to the world, the monk was a continual scandal to his fellow priests. His superior tried in vain to attract the straying sheep back to the fold of monastic discipline. Kindness proved as useless as severity. There remained only one hope, that the Infant so revered and loved by the Carmelites might work a miracle of grace for him. The superior proposed a program of community prayer for that intention; Mass was celebrated for him before the holy image. The result of these spiritual suffrages has a parallel from Holy Scripture in the story of that Egyptian king who sought to seduce the beautiful Sara. Before he could carry out his lustful design, the Lord struck him with an illness that, besides threatening his life, removed from him all such sensual desires. The Divine Physician cured the man by turning away from him the evil that, once committed, would have been a great obstacle to its cure. It has been the way of the Lord, at times, to afflict the body of man in order to save his soul. Sometimes he permits an early death to assure eternal life to a man. So it happened in this case.

The Infant Jesus dealt somewhat similarly with this stubborn, unruly priest who seemed determined to leave off striving to live in grace. Once the promised suffrages had been made as his superior promised, the tempted monk, who till this time had enjoyed the best of health, became a victim of high fever following an infection that localized in his leg. Complications set in to place the patient in grave danger of dying. Brought to his deathbed, the sinner was favored with the will to repent. What he realized was his last confession of sin became the promise of new life, spiritually speaking. Sincerely repentant and at peace with God, fortified by the last rites of the Church, he spent the last day of life on April 30, 1639.

XV

PRAGUE IS SAVED FROM ITS SWEDISH INVADERS

Militia est vita hominis super terram. Christ speaking through His evangelist warns man that his life here on this earth is a continual warfare. *Surget gens contra gentem, et regnum adversus regnum.* The history of mankind proves His words, that people will rise against people and one empire against the other.

During certain years of her past history, Bohemia seemed oblivious to the fact that the prophet was including her also in his prediction of renewed wars among the kingdoms of the earth. But she came to experience the painful truth in dealing with the Swedes, led by General Panyr (Banner) who made a surprise attack at her city gates on August 29, 1639. Unprepared to resist successfully, the people of Prague had no choice but to see their city invaded, and themselves left to struggle without the help of the nobility, who made hasty preparations to evacuate with the royal crown and treasures of state into some place of safety.

The Carmel in Prague felt its moral responsibility to lead the defenseless people to place their confidence in God in this new emergency. As his first order, the Prior insisted that the image of the Infant be transported out of its niche in the church to the monastery choir, where the monks could visualize the image, and send up their petitions for relief from the impending siege. Besides these common prayers, the monks were permitted to express their private devotion in whatever way they wished. Some of them remained to spend an all-night vigil before the little image. They pledged their lives if need be, to defend Him against the invading army should it succeed in plundering the city. If the city and its inhabitants should be spared the anticipated occupation, the divine Infant was promised a special house of veneration, where for generations he could be praised for his protection of the city and its Catholic inhabitants. A miraculous turn of events showed how pleasing were these prayers of petition.

With the break of day after the night of prayerful vigil, certain sentinels managed to break through in the direction of the enemy encampment. To their utter astonishment, not a single soldier could be seen. To all appearances the enemy army had vanished. Bohemian prisoners of war later told that General Panyr had been visited by a messenger of unknown identity, bearing a message the commander never divulged. Whatever the nature of the news, it was disturbing enough to change the general's strategy and the proposed attack was called off. The event of his retreat was a damaging one to his military career. It was an imprudent and foolish decision to act on the advice of a stranger, withdrawing his troops not only from Prague but from the whole of Bohemia.

This deliverance of Prague from the occupation of Sweden the monks of Carmel attributed to the mercy of their little Infant, known thereafter as the savior of the city.

XVI

EMPEROR FERDINAND AND THE SIEGE OF REGENSBURG—1641

With the Swedes withdrawn beyond the boundaries of their kingdom, the Bohemians were ready to rejoice with the prophet Ezechiel: *Pax, Pax!* No longer was the peace of the Holy Roman Empire in imminent danger. But Almighty God with His foreknowledge and wisdom decided differently in the council of His providence, and by clear warnings made known *"et non est pax."* It was as if the Lord were not satisfied with the people of Prague. You come to Me in your danger, He seemed to reproach them, when you are in the state of siege from your enemy. You have not held up your hands like Moses until Amalec was conquered once and for all. And because you have not persevered in prayer, there is no peace.

The truth of these words became suddenly very evident. True, the Swedish army had left hastily, and the kingdom of Bohemia experienced a miraculous manifestation of protective power through the Infant Jesus. But with the passing of the danger, there also passed the enthusiasm that characterized the allegiance of the people of Prague to its king and savior. It seemed that for their forgetfulness of His favor, the Lord provided another trial to punish this neglect and restore their former devotion.

Regensburg was the scene of a meeting of the

Diet held in February of the year 1641. Present there to discuss ways and means of establishing peace were His Majesty, Emperor Ferdinand III, the Empress Maria, Her Serene Highness, the Emperor's brother, Prince Leopold, delegates of the electorate, and various princes and representatives of the Holy Roman Empire. The weather was altogether unfavorable for any such convocation: The winter lingered on, bitter cold, and the Danube river was still choked with ice. The imperial army, moreover, was now scattered widely, and immobile in winter quarters. Travel through the empire was dangerous but undisturbed. Highroads throughout the country could be traveled unquestioned.

What an opportunity this afforded the enemy! The imperial house of Austria, even the whole of the Holy Roman Empire, lay unprotected, a prey to schemes of further invasion. General Panyr quickly took advantage of the situation to encircle the city of Regensburg. With the news of their danger came the realization that here in Regensburg were gathered the nobles of the country, together with their royal majesties, and that the Crown of the Empire faced the greater danger in the possibility of their death or captivity. The hope for help or reinforcements for the city garrison seemed almost nil.

The emperor acted immediately, sending word of their plight to his lord high steward, Henry Liebsteinsky von Kolowrat. The runner begged Prince Kolowrat to inform the Discalced Carmelites in Prague of their critical predicament. His majesty, of course, had been informed of the miraculous help they had been able to secure from the divine Infant in the liberation of Prague during the siege of the previous year. His Majesty vowed that if he and his nobles were spared this present danger, he would present himself at the shrine of the merciful Infant and dedicate himself to the little King.

Alerted to the danger confronting the imperial party, Father Prior ordered his monks to transport the image to the monastery choir. Once again the Carmelites began their intercessory vigil before the shrine. The imperial army, using its own strategem and the aid of powerful prayer, put to rout the troops of Panyr on March 11, 1641. After this defeat, the Swedish Commander ended his life unhappily and in disgrace on May 10.

Out of the Regensburg crisis comes this account of a favor granted to the high steward of the kingdom of Bohemia, the aforementioned Henry Liebsteinsky. Realizing the danger to his estates by confiscation during the anticipated invasion, this official turned in confidence to the Infant who had granted a cure several years before to his wife, Elizabeth Kolowrat. He promised an offering of one hundred ducats upon information that his lands were clear of enemy occupation troops. To obtain this favor he joined the Carmelites in person praying before the shrine of the Infant in Prague. As the welcome news reached him of the Swedish retreat from Regensburg, he laid the pledged donation at the Infant's feet.

XVII

THE INFANT IS ENSHRINED IN OUR LADY OF VICTORY CHURCH

Jephte returning victorious from the defeat of the Ammonites hastened to make good his vow to the Lord. In the event of a glorious victory he vowed to sacrifice by fire the first person who would meet him upon his return home. His pain was exceedingly great, the ancient historian notes, when that person chanced to be his beloved daughter. (Judges 11:30)

With the recent memory of a great victory won against the heretic, the time seemed opportune for Father Prior to carry out his promise to erect a shrine where the increased number of devotees of the Infant might worship Him publicly. Although the privations of the war years, the poverty of the monastery, and the lack of funds due to fewer wealthy benefactors militated against such a building program, Father Prior, though he could not deny the obstacles materially speaking, was unshakable in his desire to build. The miracle of the needed funds came about through the visitation to Father Cyril of a deceased friend of Carmel whose name will not be given here. After such visitation had occurred several times, Father Cyril addressed the visitant at the advice of his Superior, receiving this answer as to the reason for its presence. "I am X," the departed soul informed him. "While living in the world I made a promise to honor the Blessed Trinity, to Whom your church is dedicated. I failed through neglect to keep this promise, and for the past fifteen years I have been suffering the pains of Purgatory. I cannot be relieved of my suffering until this money which I vowed can be made available from my earthly estate and used for the glory of God."

When Father Cyril investigated the case, the story was confirmed by the widow of the deceased, who acknowledged her husband had made such a promise. She agreed to carry out her husband's wishes and placed three thousand florins in trust for the monastery. The first plan was to use it to construct a separate building to enshrine the holy image of the Infant. Father Prior reconsidered, deeming it more in keeping with the wishes of the benefactor to erect a new main altar in the church. Dedicated to the Holy Trinity, the altar would be surmounted by a suitable shrine, housing the Infant for all to see and venerate. Such a plan fulfilled both promises, for it would provide at the same time veneration of the Infant and expression of honor to the Blessed Trinity.

Thus in 1641 was the Infant honored, placed above the high altar of Our Lady of Victory over a gold tabernacle donated by Count Lobkowitz.

XVIII

BENEFACTIONS MULTIPLY WITH INCREASED VENERATION

The reader of the scriptural account of our Lord's public life is struck with the fact that it is never difficult for persons to approach our Savior. In fact, he never waits to be requested for favors; He grants them freely and often before they are expressed in words. Thus did He deal with the woman of Samaria. He foresaw that her only motive in coming to the well that day was to draw water for her physical well-being. Yet He waited there for her, ready to offer her something more precious—the living water of His divine mercy and promise of eternal life.

Once the Infant had been removed from behind monastery walls to the high altar for public veneration, one benefactor after the other vied for the honor of adding to the beauty and magnificence of his new throne. Not satisfied that her husband's estate had supplied the funds for the altar, the widow of X (whose story we related in the previous chapter) contributed at her own expense the massive silver lamp that hangs before it. To be used in making sacred vestments, she donated the precious brocade of her wedding gown, a token of her personal love and devotion to the Infant. Not to be outdone in generosity, Lady Febronia Pernstyn came forward with the request to pay for the inlaying of the floor of the shrine with red and white marble. Soon afterwards Lady Anna Polyxena Slavata, the Countess of Michna, offered to beautify the sanctuary by erecting a side altar in honor of the Blessed Mother of the Infant. Her gift was matched in money to erect a similar shrine to St. Joseph on the opposite side, by the Honorable John Conrad Kropff, judge of the court of appeals in Altendorf.

Other benefactors included a certain Lady Brunetta, who donated a thousand florins for a perpetual vigil light to burn before the shrine as an expression of gratitude for spiritual favors. Two other members of the Kolowrat-Pernstyn families repeated benefactions to the amount of three thousand, three hundred florins, for use in the new construction of the Carmel of Prague.

XIX

CONSTRUCTION IS BEGUN ON THE NEW SHRINE IN PRAGUE

Most of the devotees of the Infant were pleased with seeing the little image displayed in a shrine over the magnificent altar. They approved the lavish expression of devotion, the gifts and exvotos and the general beautification of the shrine. Others were dissatisfied for scrupulous reasons. Had not a vow been taken to provide the Infant with a new house of worship? Was it the entirely proper thing to place the image directly over the tabernacle? The solution to the problem was found in a mystical experience reported by Father Cyril of the Mother of God.

It was the eve of the feast of the Immaculate Conception, 1638, that Father Cyril first begged the Blessed Mother to provide her divine Infant with a suitable place for veneration. Deeply absorbed in his meditation on the mystery of the Incarnation, he was alone in the oratory. In fifteen minutes—the hour of midnight—his fellow monks would assemble there to chant the office in Our Lady's honor. Suddenly he was impelled to lift his eyes upward where a misty cloud, shot through with stars, gradually assumed a shape he recognized as the radiant Queen of Heaven. He watched enraptured as the lovely apparition lifted her arms above her head, embracing as it were the spot which she indicated would please her most as the shrine for her Infant's veneration.

Before informing his Superior of this experience, Father Cyril searched the premises and found a spot which seemed to correspond in location and availability for the shrine Our Lady had so clearly indicated during his vision. With the Prior's approval he began then to look for friends whose generosity could make the erection of the new shrine a reality. He found such a person in Benigna Catherine Belira, Baroness of Lobkowitz, wife of the custodian of the King's hunting reserves. He found in her an enthusiastic helper, honored and willing to assume the responsibility of housing the Infant in a shrine approved by Our Lady.

The Baroness spared no expense in furnishing the new shrine. Her gift of a thousand florins completely transformed the place selected into a chapel which became the first one dedicated solely to the honor of the Infant Jesus of Prague.

XX

THE BENEFACTRESS RECEIVES HER REWARD

When he arrived in the city of Naim our Blessed Lord was met with a funeral cortege. Here a widowed mother mourned her only son, and noting her deep sorrow Jesus was moved to compassion. Approaching the coffin he commanded the bearers to stand, and with a word to the deceased he restored him to life and gave him back to his mother. Recall that in this case, there had been no request for such a miracle. It was a spontaneous and sympathetic gesture on the part of Our Savior. Jesus knows the depths of a mother's love and knows, therefore, the depths of the grief which can tear her heart when that child is taken by death. There is no way of measuring the joy that filled this mother's soul when her son, no longer dead, joined her in thanking the Master of life and death.

Another widow, Baroness Lobkowitz, was witness to a similar miracle in the spiritual order worked for her only living son, Christopher Ferdinand. It was this benefactress, it will be remembered, who erected the first chapel in honor of the Infant. Her first great personal trial came through the loss of her husband in death, after which a more intolerable pain was inflicted through the scandalous conduct of her son. Because of his misdeeds she was faced with the loss of her ancestral home, and the family reputation as well.

But the compassionate Infant to whom she had showed such generous devotion rewarded her. In all her anxiety over her wayward son, she never doubted that the Infant would console her in this affliction, and eventually effect the salvation of her son. Touched by the tenderness of the mother's love and the deep spiritual concern she persisted in expressing for him, the son at last consented to make his peace with God. He received the sacraments of penance and Holy Eucharist with signs of sincere compunction and fervent amendment. After which he put this vow into writing:

Ex Voto

On this, the feast day of St. John the Baptist, I, the undersigned, hereby declare that I will provide one hundred and eighty florins yearly from my personal income for the beloved Infant Jesus at the Discalced Carmelite Monastry in Less Side, Prague, this declaration to be shown to the Carmelites and its contents guaranteed by:

(Signed) Christopher Ferdinand
Baron of Lobkowitz

(Dated) June 24, 1643

This document he placed at the feet of the image of the Infant after which he returned to his home expressing a feeling of relief and freedom from worry, filled with a new hope he had thought impossible. Hardly had a day passed when a tide of circumstances began which ended in the sparing of his reputation and his life. Often he could be found before the shrine of the Infant, pouring out his gratitude.

XXI

A SICK CHILD IS RESTORED TO HEALTH BUT HIS PARENTS MERIT PUNISHMENT

Moses, the faithful servant of God, was commanded by that divine Architect to "build a throne of mercy from purest gold, three and a half ells long and one and a half ells wide." Such minute measurement might cause one to ponder: Almighty God, is not all perfection Yours? Why then do you command a one-half ell of imperfection to be included in Your perfect work? With St. Bruno we might well answer: God is a Throne of mercy, in which one finds fractions of measures and of half measures, since the Lord is both merciful and just at one and the same time. He deals out, as He wills, either mercy or justice.

How significant this observation becomes as we consider how the Infant Jesus, enthroned now on a seat of mercy in His new chapel, deals out grace and punishment, mercy and justice, according as His wisdom dictates.

The point is brought closer home in the story of a noble couple of the house of Lobkowitz. His Excellency Adam Udalrick, Baron Poppel and Anna Maria Poppeline, the Baroness of Sternberg, were the noble parents of an only child, a son, who they hoped would become the consolation and the support of their old age. In His far-seeing justice, God saw fit to spare them their son, because of their prayerful pleas for his life.

The little lad's illness was of such a nature that physicians gave his parents scant hope of saving his life. They stood by helplessly, unable to alleviate his suffering. The realization of the impotency of human help inspired them to act quickly through a spiritual channel. Their first thought was of the throne of mercy, the chapel dedicated to the Infant (the gift of the sick child's paternal grandmother). The father traveled to the monastery in Prague, where he made a vow. He pleaded for the health of his little son, promising a votive offering of two thousand florins for the upkeep of the shrine. *Vade, filius tuus vivit.* He might have heard these words of the divine Physician, for while he prayed, the sick child began to regain strength and in a short time was his normal self again. The attending physicians noted his case with astonishment, and agreed that the cure was beyond normal means.

Thus far we have seen manifested the mercy of the Infant; but His justice also had a part to play in the history of this miraculous cure. The father of the child restored to health put off the fulfillment of his promise, mainly through neglect and procrastination. This conduct did not go unnoticed or unpunished by the Infant, and only when the child was again afflicted and gave signs of his former state of health did the parent repent his fault. This time he put the promise into writing, signed and sealed in the presence of the holy image. Upon arrival home the crisis had passed, and the child played happily about his home, a proof of the ready forgiveness merited by a repentant heart.

But great is the fickleness of human nature. The father once more engrossed in worldly business deferred again the fulfillment of his vow. His own sudden death seems to have been the price of his neglect and ingratitude. This was followed by the death of son, whose passing he had begged so fervently of the Infant to postpone. This double sorrow for a time was forgotten by the widowed mother through remarriage, but her new joy was short-lived, ending in her sudden and unexpected death.

XXII

A CHILDLESS COUPLE ARE BLESSED WITH AN HEIR

Is there anything too wonderful for the Lord? The question is asked in *Genesis* in the course of the story which details the announcement to Abraham of the birth of a son and heir. Three strangers, who intimated by their knowledge of the name Sara (though they had not yet seen Abraham's wife) that they were more than ordinary men, predicted that she would bear a son, though she was long barren. At which prediction Sara laughed, "Shall I indeed bear a child, though I am old?"

(Gen. 18:12) Yet the blessed event as the Lord foretold it came to pass in the person of Isaac, the root of whose name contains the idea of laughter. And Sara unable to restrain her joy, invited others to rejoice with her saying, *"Risi fecit mihi Deus, quicumque audierit, corridebit mihi."* (God has given me laughter, and whoever hears me will laugh with me.)

Such a cause for rejoicing has its counterpart in the lives of a noble couple named Diffenbach, who were granted a male heir through the power of the Infant Jesus.

By the year 1644 the fame of the cures and other favors wrought through the Infant had spread beyond the boundaries of Bohemia into Austria. The Baroness von Sternberg, Lady Elizabeth Diffenbach, and her husband, Rudolph Baron Diffenbach, grieved that they had no child to lavish their affections on, and no male heir to inherit their fortune. The couple had almost reconciled themselves to being childless when the Lady Elizabeth heard of miraculous favors originating from the shrine in Prague. She sent an offering of two hundred florins to the monastery there, requesting prayers that God might send them a son to perpetuate the family name. The birth of a son within the year became the cause of great rejoicing. Nothing is impossible to God, an angel had once declared to Zachary, aged like this child's father. In grateful thanks he added a gift of thirty-three florins to the former donation. Frequently thereafter the Diffenbach family visited the Infant's shrine in Prague. Their offer to finance the building of a new monastery on their family estate in Jicin, Bohemia, could not, for practical reasons be accepted by the Carmelite Fathers, though they deeply appreciated the generous offer.

XXIII
CHRONIC ILLNESS IS RELIEVED AND A DANGER AVERTED

The history of severe headaches is almost as old as mankind itself. A biblical account in the fourth book of *Kings* (4:19) concerns a young boy whose birth had been foretold by Eliseus. *Caput meum doleo!* On a certain day when he went out with his father to the reapers, he complained: "My head acheth, my head acheth." The father, sympathetic but unable to help the sufferer, ordered him taken to his mother (the Sunamitress whose hospitality Eliseus had enjoyed), who "set him on her knees until noon, and then he died." (4 Kings, 420). Fortunately for her, Eliseus that "man of God" she requested to come again, performed the desired miracle, and the boy lived again.

The case of the devout Eva Febronia Perenthal had almost reached the crisis of death when she betook herself to that healer, of whom the Evangelist says He radiates the power to heal. Bedridden for months, plagued by severe headaches for which she had vainly sought a cure, Eva Perenthal promised an offering to the divine Infant and reception of the sacraments for the intention, if it pleased God, to be relieved of her illness. Immediately she began to notice a change; she insisted, even in her weakened condition, on being conveyed by carriage to the Infant's shrine. Here she kept her promise leaving behind ex-votos in a set of cruets plated with gold for use at Mass, and a silver water basin, and other precious items.

XXIV

THE INFANT PREVENTS THE LOSS OF PRECIOUS JEWELS

Rich or poor, we are all children of our Heavenly Father. Why then do some suffer poverty and great need, while others enjoy wealth in abundance? Why did Christ warn, *"Voe vobis divitibus!"* Woe to you rich! Is it not for the reason that God in His wisdom has provided the poor with an opportunity to earn, through patience, and conversely for the wealthy, an opportunity to detach their hearts from riches through charity? There is wisdom in the psalmist's words, *"Divitae si affluant, nolite cor apponere."* One who receives riches, ought not hang his heart on them. Wealth, as the prophet Daniel teaches, affords an opportunity to expiate sin: *"Peccata tua elemosynis redime."* This recommendation to "redeem sin by gifts" has a fitting application in a family of aristocratic rank whose name it were better not to mention here.

The family in question were among the inhabitants of Brno, the capital of Moravia, when it was under siege by the Swedish war lord, General Borstenson. The year was 1645, and the heavy bombardment that fell during a concerted attack by the enemy would have forced the city to capitulate had it not been for the protective arm of the Lord, who worked a miracle in its behalf.

But before the liberation, what fearful hours our nobleman spent, concerned for his worldly possessions! A fortune in jewels and gold and silver he considered all but lost, and with them the means to continue the benefactions others had come to expect of his charity. Realizing the powerlessness of human help in this circumstance, he sought the intercession of One Who became poor Himself out of great love for man. Before word finally came of Brno's liberation from siege, the divine Infant had been promised votive gifts: a gold-embroidered chasuble, a gold chain studded with precious jewels, and four brass candelabras. The prayers were not in vain. As the distraught nobleman continued in prayer, word came that the enemy had been forced to withdraw. The city, almost in enemy possession, was suddenly abandoned, a prey to the ravages of continuous rain, and the prospect of sharing the aftermath of hunger and disease. The enemy troops counted themselves fortunate to leave, for all their heavy losses. The nobleman's wealth was found intact, and the charity it effected proved the owner's gratitude to the divine Infant.

XXV

HIGH RANKING PERSONS CONTINUE TO BE FAVORED

"Vidimus stellam ejus." A star in the heavens led the Magi to search for the Messias. We have seen His star, they said, and following its direction they came to Bethlehem and the Child. Another person, Herod, also sought the presence of the Child. Where, he asked the Scribes of Jerusalem, could one hope to find the Messias? Bethlehem of Juda, he was told, but the scriptures make it clear that King Herod made no move to act upon this information with the idea of going there to worship the Messias. He heard, but he did not see. He heard concerning the sign of the Messias, but like the scribes who informed him, he could believe only what his eyes could see and his hands touch. The Magi showed the greater wisdom. In the star they saw the great sign, and their faith brought its own great reward, the person of the divine Child Himself.

Many men of this world, reputed wise, suffer from the folly of Herod and the scribes. They have been informed about the Infant Jesus. They have heard of His ready grace and incomparable mercy displayed in miracles. But their eyes of faith remain blind, and their minds incredulous. Their refusal to worship the Child militates against them and they suffer the ill effects of such disbelief all their lives long.

To those who believe are given many additional

gifts. The devotees of the Infant by the year 1645 had so grown in number that to recount all the remarkable incidents occurring at the Shrine in Prague would be almost endlessly long. We shall confine ourselves, therefore, to only the outstanding events recorded.

This is the case, for example, of His Grace, Baron Christopher Vratislav. This Bohemian official, the royal chamberlain and official to the Court of Petty Sessions, on one of his visits to Prague felt compelled to visit the chapel where, he was told, wonderful things had been happening. So impressed was he with the sight of the lovely Infant that his heart rejoiced much as the Psalmist, whose canticle he borrowed: *Speciosus forma prae filiis hominum, diffusa est gratia in labiis tuis* (You are most beautiful in form before the children of men; grace flows from your lips.) So ardent was his devotion to the divine Child that he never missed the consolation of weekly confession and Holy Communion. A regular visitor to the shrine, he left as proof of his devotedness the sum of a thousand, one hundred and sixty-six florins. Truly the fire of true love is unquenchable; it endures beyond this life. Baron Vratislav's last will and testament added another five hundred florins to the testament of his devotion to the Infant.

A second nobleman, Baron Johannes Kaffla, was a frequent visitor to the chapel of the miraculous image. This "Abraham" of Prague, this "Elias" of Bohemia, as he has been called, never tired in busying himself in the service of God. In testimony of his devotion, Baron Kaffla left the record of numerous benefactions during his lifetime, and at death, willed the monastery two hundred florins in honor of the Infant.

XXVI

AN INHERITANCE IS RESTORED AND THE GIFT OF SOLNICE MADE TO OUR MONASTERY

Holy Scripture relates the story of two women who disputed the title of mother before the throne of the wise King Solomon. Each claimed the living child as her own, disclaiming the dead one found smothered in its sleep. The wise judge announced that the child must be shared, cut in half to satisfy both women. The real mother proved herself; she begged that the little one's life be spared, and that he be given to the other woman, who had agreed to Solomon's proposal. *Date huic infantum vivum haec est mater ejus!* The judgment is well known: Give the child alive to this one, for she is his mother. (3 Kings 3:16.)

Not so generally known is the fact that when Solomon pronounced this judgment he was standing before the Ark of the Covenant, offering a sacrifice to God.

There is a lesson to be learned from this, and an application can be made in a story related about Lady Febronia Pernstyn.

Upon the death of her brother, Vratislav Baron

Pernstyn, Lady Febronia Eusebia Baroness Pernstyn became the legal heir to thirty thousand florins. This amount had accrued on a loan made during the difficult war years by her brother to Emperor Ferdinand II, a mortgage on the Solnice estate. It was a case that proved the ancient proverb: Where money jingles, many gather to dance and sing. There came forward others claiming to be legal heirs, urging a settlement if not in full, for each of them a part, something like the living child dispute of our scriptural story. The wrangling grew until Lady Febronia, the sole and rightful heir, was faced with the danger of bankruptcy. Moreover, the royal chamber was so embarrassed, due to the multitude of claimants, that there was question indeed if any should receive payment. Despairing of human help, Lady Febronia presented her case to a wise and just Solomon, the Judge of all things—the Infant King. In gratitude she promised to donate to the Carmelites whatever monetary settlement would come of the case.

Within fifteen days of her decision, Baroness Pernstyn was informed of the imperial decree that declared her the sole legal heir to the Solnice lands, ordering all debts due the estate payable to her. Thereafter, she referred to the property in Solnice as the "estate of the Infant Jesus."

How generously Lady Febronia sacrificed for the honor of the Infant recalls the greater sacrifice demanded by God of Abraham. "Since you have done this, and have not withheld your only son, I will indeed bless you, and will surely multiply your descendants." (Gen. 22:15). But you may ask, have not others besides Abraham pleased the Lord with sacrifice? Yes, but God is most pleased when we sacrifice that which is dearest to us, as this father did his only son. Note that God did not simply command, "Take your only son." He added significantly, "Whom you love, and offer him as a holocaust on the hill which I shall point out to you." (Gen. 22:2).

But to the confused children of this earth, treasures and riches are the "only begotten son." Very few are willing to make the sacrifice of this son to their creator, the giver of all gifts. The opportunity for them to do so is close at hand; they could sacrifice by means of gift-giving and the making of foundations. But no, more deeply interested in the unnatural son, their riches, they pay but little concern for their soul's salvation. They seem to forget that the more it is deeply rooted in the heart, the more strongly attached they are to their gift, the more acceptable is that gift to God.

Lady Febronia in her generous conduct could be said to rival Abraham. The Solnice estate was hers through the goodness of God; she gave it to our monastery in Prague out of the goodness of her heart, for the love of the litte Infant. Surely she has merited to hear the promise of reward for selflessness. For He has said: *"Omnia relinquerit domun, centuplum recipiet, et vitam æternam possidabit."* Whoever relinguishes his possessions shall receive a hundredfold and shall possess life everlasting.

XXVII

THOSE WHO TRUST THE INFANT WILL FIND A GOOD FATHER

Sometimes we hear complaints about religious superiors that they fail to exercise sufficient vigilance and care over their communities. More often than not, such complaints are unfounded. However anxious and careful men may be, they work in vain if God is not with them. As the Psalmist puts it: *"Nisi Dominus custodierit eam."* Where the Lord does not watch over the city, whosoever watches it, watches in vain. Human care alone, for example, is not sufficient in the matter of providing food. *"Jacta super Dominun curam tuam et ipse te anutriet,"* we are told by David. Entrust our cares to the Infant Jesus, therefore, and we shall find in Him a vigilant and generous provider.

When the newly appointed Prior arrived at the monastery in Prague in 1642, he demonstrated this trust by ordering the image of the Holy Infant to be brought into the choir during his installation ceremonies. "My beloved Jesus," he said, addressing the Infant, "You know my unworthiness and incompetence for this office. Therefore I place Thee, beloved Infant, in my place here as Prior of this monastery. To you I give this key; I place all administrative care into Your hands." And now consider how wonderously the Infant Jesus governed as the head of his religious family.

The year that followed was one in which God

severely put His Carmelite servants to trial. Their trial only emphasized the more the light and gracious help of the Infant Jesus, and attracted many others to His loving service. First of all, the vineyards offered little hope of a harvest, due partly to lack of money to invest in its cultivation and partly to the blight that had resulted from a frost. Things continued to grow worse, until the monks suffered keenly from the misery of impoverishment. Furthermore, the Carmelites became involved in a lawsuit involving the ownership of the Solnice estate. There was reason to fear that the case might end in favor of rival secular claimants who had more influence in the courts.

In this critical situation, the Prior turned confidently to the Infant, whom shortly before he had invested with the right and powers of administering the affairs of his monastery. He commissioned Father Cyril to represent their community intention in prayer to the Infant. Obediently the monk poured out his petition, and heard these words! "Do not worry, but seek first the kingdom of God and His justice, and you shall have plenty. Serve me faithfully, and I will do the same for you." This divine direction was followed, with the result that the monks were "speedily delivered from all material need," as their Prior testified in writing. Without being cultivated, and despite their frostbitten condition, the monks' vineyards began to yield abundantly, even before their neighbors' did. The farms of Solnice supplemented the needs of the community, and best of all, this estate was guaranteed them by a favorable judgment that came of the impending lawsuit. There was great rejoicing in Carmel over these favors. Personally and in the name of his monks the superior praised the power of the Infant, "May His name be blessed forever," he prayed, "for showing us the wonders of His paternal care. Amen."

XXVIII

FERDINAND III VISITS THE SHRINE TO FULFILL HIS PROMISE

Jerusalem was in the state of siege, and King Ezechias lamented the prospect of King Sennacharib conquering the city. But the Lord comforted him through the prophet Isaias. He was told to have no fear that Sennacharib would enter the city, for "I will save this city because of David," said the Lord. That God should save a city out of consideration for a faithful servant is not difficult to understand. That is, it is not difficult to those who trust God's power to protect them in time of danger. And did these kings—the recipients of that merciful power—express their gratitude? *Reges videbunt et adorabunt propter Dominum, quis fidelis est, consurgent Principes, et adorabunt propter Dominum, quis fidelis est,* prophesied Isaias. Because the Lord is true, such a king did arise to worship Him in the person of Ferdinand III.

The Sennacharib of our day—General Panyr—besieged the city of Regensburg, as we mentioned in a preceding chapter, reducing that city to a state of desolation. Yet there remained this hope: their Emperor had sought the aid of the Infant in a previous crisis. To the besieged people this fact seemed a reassurance that Panyr would indeed enter the city, but leave as quickly as he had come.

Their hopes were verified. This was the year Ferdinand had planned to visit the city to fulfill his vow. Publicly he knelt at the feet of the beloved image and placed his votive offering: forty candles of purest wax, a tribute from Venice. This act of allegiance on the Emperor's part, if it did nothing else, set an example for the faithful of Prague to place their hope of deliverance in the Infant.

XXIX

THE PRIOR IS SAVED FROM CRITICAL ILLNESS

The story of Christ's benefactions as a Physician is well known. The case of the captain's servant is to the point. As he had done before for Zacheus, Christ blessed the centurion's house. But note the difference. This latter blessing benefited only the patient therein; the whole household of Zacheus had been recipients. *Sanatus est puer,* Christ assured the captain. We might explain the difference in these two incidents by pointing out the deep faith of Zacheus, a son of Abraham. But did not Christ Himself remark the deep faith of the centurion? *Non inveni tantam fidem in Israel.* Such deep faith as this I have not found in Israel. (Luke 7:9). By way of explaining the distinction between the two cases we may be justified to say this: Christ entered the house of Zacheus in person, blessing it as He did so with the promise: *"Salus huic domui est."* Whereas in the case of the servant cured, he entered the house not at all, because his master, the centurion, demonstrated faith that merited the cure without Christ's presence.

Today is salvation come to this house. The Prior of our monastery in Prague had personal reason to say this of his monastery because of his own miraculous cure. Seized one night with sudden excruciating pain, he was unable to see or speak. The condition could not be relieved, and the physician's verdict was that there could be little hope of recovery. The patient indicated by signs that he wanted the image of the Infant brought to his bedside. Almost immediately the desperately ill Prior began to respond to the divine Physician. He insisted, moreover, that the image remain in his room until his complete return to health. This occurred within a few days. In gratitude he marched with his monks in solemn procession, as they bore back the little King to His chapel throne, where Holy Mass was celebrated in thanksgiving. As further expressions of their gratitude the Carmelites supplied a precious new chalice and a censer for liturgical services.

XXX

THE INFANT JESUS STRENGTHENS THE OLD AND INFIRM

There are important lessons for us all to learn from the conduct of our great Master and Teacher, Jesus Christ. St. Luke sets forth the prescriptions of a host on the matter of selecting guests for a great dinner. "When you prepare a feast, do not invite the rich only, and your relatives and friends, but ask the poor, the crippled, the lame, the blind." (Luke 14:12.) By his counsel in this matter, Christ took the opportunity to reprimand those who consider the very presence of the rich and powerful an honor, and reproach those who entertain guests in the hopes of securing some later benefits from them. Christ condemns this kind of conduct: *Voca pauperas debiles, caecos.* And if you do invite the poor and the feeble and the blind, do not expect, He says, to have your reward here on this earth. Only in Heaven can the "Blessed of My Father" expect to have their charity rewarded. "Come, take possession of the kingdom prepared for you from the foundation of the world. For I was hungry and you fed Me; thirsty and you gave Me to drink; I was a stranger and you took Me in; naked and you covered Me; sick and you visited Me; I was in prison and you came to Me." (Matt. 25:35)

In a previous chapter we recalled how our beloved Infant invited the poor to His feast and helped them plentifully. To the blind, He gave sight; to the mute, their speech; the sick He restored to health. In the following account it is an infirm old man who recovers his strength. The miraculous happening he himself reported under oath to all the monks. The gentleman in question was a county judge, the Honorable John Adam Smickowsky, who testifies:

"When the time came for final judgment in the Solnice estate, I had the greatest share of the work to do, namely, notifying officials and counselors and briefing them as to details. I am old and the burden of this work took all my physical strength. I became so weak I was unable to carry on. This was endangering the outcome of the suit. In this pitiful condition I prayed to our gracious Infant Jesus for help and made a vow. Almost immediately, to my amazement, my health was restored. I was able to bring my work to a favorable end. Ideas which contributed to the happy outcome of the suit came into my mind with little or no mental labor. For this reason I came to worship the gracious Infant Jesus, my Savior, and fulfill my promise to Him."

With this statement the judge left an ex-voto of five hundred florins, to which his wife added another five hundred, to be spent for the honor of the Infant Jesus.

XXXI
A STUTTERER RECOVERS FROM HIS SPEECH IMPAIRMENT THROUGH THE INFANT

There are times in our lives when we ought to blame ourselves for much of our misery, but hesitate to do so because of self-love. Often in the history of cities has the Lord sent hardships because of the sinful lives of their inhabitants. No one, of course, can doubt that the innocent suffer also, as the case of the man born blind, of whom Christ said, *"Neque hic peccavit, neque parentes ejus, ut manifestentur opera Dei in illo."* Neither this man nor his parents have sinned, but for the manifestation of the hand of the Lord. The answer may be a consolation in the lives of you who have had to suffer various afflictions. The case of Count Philip Mansfeldt may serve to recall that affliction can lead one to recognize the miraculous power of the Infant Jesus.

Philip Mansfeldt, military commandant, traveled in 1647 from Vienna to Prague on imperial business. While in Prague he became critically ill, a hopeless case according to his personal physician. The sick man, however, never gave up hope of recovery and promised if spared, to have several Holy Masses read in the chapel where the Infant is enshrined. Restored to health much to the amazement of his doctors, he was able to travel to the shrine and leave there his promised offering of twelve ducats. And there is an additional favor reported about him, as we shall see.

The Count was commonly known to stutter so painfully that his speech was often unintelligible, a defect which marred the success of an otherwise successful army career. Embarrassed and distressed because of this impediment, he prayed before the miraculous image to be delivered, remembering the words of Solomon: "Wisdom has opened the mouth of the mute and made the tongues of the children talk." *Sapiente aperuit os mutuorum et linguas infantium fecit disertas.* Full of hope after receiving the sacraments for this intention, the Count returned to the court in Vienna to report on the business to which he had been commissioned. He amazed himself and all who were listening. The emperor, commenting on his eloquence, praised also his wisdom and honored him with the office of privy counselor. In gratitude Count Mansfeldt asked permission to hang a silver lamp in the chapel at Prague, and left there a donation of thirty-three florins, in honor of the thirty-three years spent on earth by the Incarnate Son of God. At the monastery he declared under oath that the favor had come through the Infant Jesus.

XXXII

INTERCESSION TO THE INFANT SETTLES A LAWSUIT FAVORABLY 1648

St. John in one of his early revelations describes Christ surrounded by seven candelabra. What, I asked myself, was the Lord's purpose in such a vision — standing among seven branches of candles? In a later vision He is described as "walking about in the middle and from one to the other." In search of the meaning of this mystery I came upon this explanation: By the seven candelabra are symbolized the judges of this earth. Jesus walks among them, cleaning and oiling them, as it were, that the light of their truth may always penetrate the darkness, that they might never fail to lead the world to justice. And what St. John saw in this mysterious vision we shall see revealed by analogy in the case of the monk, Father Joseph Maria, a Carthusian from Jicin, who was conducting a difficult litigation involving his Order.

The case had been a long-drawn-out one, over which the judges — the lights of the candelabra we mentioned above — were unable to pass judgment. Periodically new complaints were registered, and fresh doubts were raised to delay the decision. In desperation, Father Joseph Maria asked for a miracle from the Infant Jesus. During Holy Mass which he offered in the shrine of the Infant, he prayed with the mind of the visionary that the Infant might walk again among the seven branches of candles, that burnished and clean, the court might see the light of truth in the case and act justly in reaching a decision. In a very short time the judge rendered an opinion that concluded the case favorably for the Order. The priest himself termed this a miraculous answer to prayer, and offered Holy Mass in thanksgiving.

XXXIII

A HOUSE OF WORSHIP IS CONSECRATED FOR THE INFANT JESUS

Holy Mother the Church prescribes the reading of the gospel narrative about Zacheus on the feast of the consecration of a church. She does this for an instructive and significant reason. "Zacheus," our Lord called up to the publican, "make haste to come down; for this day I plan to stay at your house." Is not Zacheus perched among the branches of a tree a symbol of the cross? *Festinando descendo, quia hodie in domo tua opertet me manere.* And why must he descend? Because I intend to be a guest at his house, and he must hasten to put all things in readiness. He must adorn his house with virtues. "Do you not know," St. Paul asks the Christian, "that you are the temple of the Lord?" Temples of the Lord are holy places. For this reason the Church is most careful to rid these places of worship of anything that will disturb, anything that is out of order there, anything that will make them less than holy.

The church where the miraculous image was enshrined had already been dedicated and solemnly blessed on the feast of the Holy Name of Jesus, January 14, 1644, with a fitting sermon and beautiful music. But in view of the fact that so many miracles had occurred there, the Prior of the monastery arranged for it to be consecrated with full ceremony, which was done on May 3, 1648. The Prince Archbishop of Prague, His Eminence Ernest Adalbert Harrach, presided on this occasion. After the celebration of the Holy Sacrifice of the Mass, all the priests, secular and religious, were given permission to offer Holy Mass at the altar of the Infant. His Eminence made a personal donation of fifty ducats in honor of the occasion. A large number of the attending clergy followed his example, and honored the Great and Little One of Prague with gifts and pledges. How well pleased was the Infant with this expression of devotion demonstrated at the consecration of His Church, we shall relate in the following chapter.

XXXIV

THE MONASTERY IS SPARED THE ATTACK OF THE SWEDES UPON LESS SIDE

The Psalmist cries out in triumph at the scene one might envision as taking place in Heaven as the angels prepare to welcome Christ at His entry on the day of His ascension from the earth. "Open wide the gates: here cometh the Lord God, the Mighty One in battle!" *Dominus virtutum ipse est Rex gloriae.* Would you know why Christ is called the Mighty Lord and the Lord of Virtue? Then hear an account that will provide this lesson: Bring first a sacrifice of virtue to God, if you expect Him to furnish you power and protection in your struggle with enemies.

A previous chapter pointed out that besides our monks, many persons of high and low degree worshipped the Infant by faith, hope, and love. Pleased with these virtues, the little Infant proved Himself a mighty Commander in their time of conflict with the Swedish enemy.

The Carmelites had just begun their morning

devotions on the feast of St. Anne on July 26, 1648, when news broke that General Koenigsmark and his troops were storming the city. It was a surprise attack in which the guards at Strahov were killed, and three thousand enemy troops were free to plunder and sack the city of Prague. Enemy bombardment shook the monastery walls as the monks were at prayer. Their first move was to hasten to the church and consume the Sacred Species in the tabernacle to prevent profanation by the heretics. Then the Community quickly organized a plan of action:

Divided into three groups, the first began a vigil of prayer and meditation to avert the danger; the second band hurried out to the gates of the city to make an attempt to dissuade the invaders from looting the monastery; the third group removed from the church all the sacred vessels to a place of safety. None of them doubted the Infant would spare them. This indeed He did; the first group of soldiers who entered the monastery left it, satisfied to receive food and drink, without any disturbance of the monastic property.

However, a second band followed almost immediately upon the departure of the first. But consider in what a remarkable way God answered the prayers of the monks! At the monastery entrance there appeared a handsome protector, sword unsheathed, ready to resist a forced entrance. As soon as this *Salva Guardia* had accomplished his mission of protection, he was seen to disappear. It is not difficult to guess the identity of this heroic stranger. Considering previous miraculous favors, there is little doubt that our little King showed Himself the Lord of Virtues, the Mighty One praised by the psalmist.

XXXV

FURTHER MIRACLES AT THE MONASTERY IN LESS SIDE PRAGUE

Consider the plight of the stricken Israelites in bondage under the cruel Pharoah, who refused to let the people of God leave Egypt. "Who is the Lord that I should hear His plea to let Israel go . . . I know not the Lord." (Ex. 5:2). But later on, the same Pharaoh, strangely subdued, begged of Aaron and Moses to do him a favor. "Leave my people at once, take the Israelites with you and begone." (Ex. 5:2).

How can this change of heart be explained? Holy Scripture gives the key to the answer, as it describes the devout Moses offering unceasing prayer to God. In this prayer lay the strength to subdue the wrath of the cruel enemy and humble an obdurate King. We can find a parallel to this protection in an incident which occurred during the conquest of the Less Side of Prague.

As emissary to the Swedish invaders, the Prior sent a lay brother with a request for protection for the monastery. The Swedish general in command of the city had a reputation for abusive language, especially when priests were referred to. It was a great surprise, therefore, when the general received the monk in a friendly, almost brotherly way, with no display of his former insolence.

Refugees of war crowded the monastery buildings with what little they could salvage from the invaders, and they received food and shelter from the Carmelites from July 27 to August 15. Impressed with this charitable service, the commanding officer of the enemy troops spoke of the monks as "our brothers" and granted their request for protection for the monastery, where a hundred sixty of the enemy, wounded during the attack on the city, were receiving medical care. Those who died of injuries had to be kept until arrangements were made for removal of the bodies. This increased the danger of contagion, but fortunately none of the monks contracted disease. They were praised for their charitable work when the Count Palatine arrived. Impressed with stories of the Infant's protection, the Swedish officer visited His shrine and left an offering of fifty ducats. He renewed the guard for the cloister, promised to remove the enemy quartered there, and ordered immediate return of books forcibly removed from the monastery library.

The Infant had been the center of constant petition during the siege and conquest of Prague. Both monks and laity attributed their safety to Him. Like Moses, who kept his arms uplifted in prayer for his people, the monks had taken turns at vigil before the holy image, supplicating the little King to spare his people. And the people of Prague followed their example; they gathered at devotions in common each morning and evening, including in their prayers the litany of the Most Holy Name of Jesus.

XXXVI

DEVOTEES OF THE INFANT ARE DELIVERED FROM THE PLAGUE

Whom God loves, these He chastises, that by suffering they may be perfected. Recall the plague that felled the Israelites under David, seventy thousand dying within hours. *Numerate populum ut sciam numerum ejus.* This had been David's order, dictated by vanity and pride. Contrast it with another edict issued by the Roman Emperor Augustus: *Exit decretum a Caesare Auguste, ut describeretur universus orbis.* There is no record of any immediate punishment coming of this. Are we to conclude, therefore, that the Lord was more grievously offended by David's pride than by the same fault in Caesar? Not at all. As later events prove, punishment for Caesar Augustus was reserved for another time. The man whom God does not punish for sin is miserable indeed. Unworthy of punishment such a man proves himself unworthy of love also. To David God showed many mercies; to the repentant sinner, God shows love and forgiveness.

The citizens of Prague could look upon the plague sent them in 1649 as a definite sign of God's chastizing love. Certainly it is permissible for a people to pray that God will spare them punishment. In this, David is the example, and God showed him mercy by ordering the avenging angel to "stay thy hand, for it is enough!"

Now that the Less Side of Prague was stricken with plague, the Prior realized that this merciless guest would soon reach out its ravaging hands into neighboring areas. He feared with good reason that it might seek admission to our own monastery, as it had already visited the Dominican Fathers. The monks shared this sense of danger with their superior. Following his example they brought their problem to the feet of the spiritual head of their community — the Infant Jesus. In petition they inaugurated the practice of a fast day followed by a High Mass offered in His honor, each priest celebrating in the presence of others who would chant aloud the litany of the Most Holy Name of Jesus.

XXXVII

THE INFANT JESUS METES OUT PUNISHMENT BY THE PLAGUE — 1649

Christ in His bitter passion willed to drain the cup of suffering to its bitter dregs. The cup of wine mixed with gall He refused, saying to his executioners: *Cum gustasset, noluit bibere.* Recall the mysterious statement to the disciples concerning the institution of the Holy Eucharist. "I say to you that I shall not drink the fruit of this wine until the day when I shall drink with you again in the kingdom of My Father." This was the solemn pledge He made, and because of it, Christ refused to drink the wine mixed with gall offered Him on Calvary. This is evidence of how He dislikes the broken promise, why He punishes those who fail to keep their vows.

The plague continued, as we related in a previous chapter, sweeping through Less Side until the monks led the people of Prague to take refuge before the image of their Infant. At the Carmel was a certain religious, Father Philip by name, who along with the other monks solemnly pledged certain prayers to the Infant. But how weak and inconstant are the resolutions of man! How urgently he pleads, but how quickly he forgets! So it happened in the case of Father Philip. He neglected to fulfill his part of the prayerful bargain, and as punishment for this fault quickly fell a victim to the plague. Critically ill, he was given the last rites. But he received also the light and grace to reflect on his obligation. Aware of his fault and contrite, the monk begged forgiveness of God and renewed his promise of prayer. A merciful thing happened: his life was spared, and within a short time of his resolution to make good his vow, every sign of all sickness left him. It was a case where, like the leper cleansed by the touch of Christ's hand, a sinner was shown great mercy. "And Jesus, having compassion on him, stretched forth His hand and touched him and said to him: 'I will; be thou made clean.' " (Mark 1:41).

XXXVIII

A SLANDERER IS DENIED ENTRANCE TO THE CHAPEL OF THE INFANT — 1649

The men who disgraced the temple of God once aroused the anger of Christ. Of these He demanded, shouting, "*Nolite facere domum Patris mei, domum negotiationis!* Make not the house of My Father a house of business." Saying this, He made a whip of cords and used it to drive the bargainers out of the temple.

At this point I am forced to consider not only the zealous wrath of our Savior, but to speculate about the whip. Was it made of rope? Yes, *Et cum fecisset quasi flagellum de funiculis omnes ejecit de templem.* Why not some other instrument of punishment, like a stick perhaps? The reason for the scourge is this: unlike the stick, the scourge uplifted to strike the offender first falls along the shoulder of the one administering the punishment. Thus Christ gives His priests a lesson not only of zeal for the glory of the house of God, but also the lesson of their personal need for mortification. Theirs is the responsibility of avoiding any cause of dishonor in themselves, lest they in turn feel the scourge of their High Priest, Jesus Christ.

The following story will emphasize this point. There came to the Carmel in Prague in 1649 a religious from the Netherlands, a Canon, who explained that he was involved in a litigation against his brother, a native of Prague. For reasons of economy and convenience, he asked permission to live at our monastery, and was given for his use a cell located near the chapel of our Infant. He preferred this part of the house, he said, for it gave him quiet and the proper atmosphere for reflecting on the business he had on hand, and a place of retreat for closer union with God. All of which was a pretense. It soon became evident that he spent most of his time dissolutely, being interested mainly in food and drink and crafty ways to win his lawsuit. The monks were indignant to see how hurriedly and with what little outward display of devotion he celebrated Holy Mass. The Infant Jesus reached for His scourge, so to speak. Three consecutive times, without explanation of how it could have happened, the priest wakened to find himself stretched across the open doorway of the chapel. Afraid of more severe punishment, the Canon humbly confessed his wrong-doing and made reparation to the Infant.

XXXIX

A BEGGAR IS RICHLY REWARDED BY THE INFANT JESUS

An analysis of the sin of our first parents involves these factors, the sinners themselves, Adam and Eve; the instrument of their sin, the serpent; and the forbidden tree itself. Of these four, only the tree escaped the wrath of God. If the serpent was cursed as an instrument of this sin why, you ask, did the tree remain unpunished? You admit that the tree, because it lacks volition, could not reasonably be blamed; but neither could the serpent, since it also acted as an instrument of the devil, lacking a will of its own. Perhaps, you suggest, the tree was spared because our first parents in their shame used its leaves to cover their nakedness. That interpretation is a worthy one. The tree of Paradise was permitted to grow and bear rich fruit. The moral of the story is that the one who gives freely and generously to those in need will escape the curse of God, and also receive his reward in this life. The story of the beggar of Solnice will illustrate this point.

Father Prior was returning to our monastery on December 22, having visited the Solnice estate, when he was approached by an attractive stranger. The young man begged for five *greschen,* asking his alms in the name of the Infant Jesus. At mention of the holy name, the Prior gave gladly to the young beggar. The gift was richly rewarded. The Solnice estate, where the monk had spent the previous few days, had proved to be a disappointment; it seemed hopeless to expect any returns from the lands within the year. Is it not a strange coincidence that just as the Prior arrived home in Prague, a remittance of ninety florins was sent in from Solnice! There seemed no explanation for the sudden unexpected returns from lands apparently so depleted except the fulfillment of the promise of Christ: *Date et dabitur vobis.* Give and thou shalt receive.

XL

THREE PRIESTS ARE RESCUED FROM MURDERERS

Ego sum, replied Jesus to His captors. And the soldiers who came into the garden to take Him prisoner were thrown to the ground by the force of these simple words. They fell twice at hearing His words, "I am He," but at the third answer to their question, they bound and led Him away. There is a lesson to be learned from this mysterious incident. Twice Christ said plainly "I am He." He repeated the words, making it plain that He was the Savior of men, that He was willing to sacrifice Himself for them. The divine power has been known to crush the enemy and liberate the faithful in other instances, such as we shall narrate concerning three of our priests.

It was March 3, 1650 and three monks were on their way to Lojovitz to secure altarbreads from Lady von Pernthal. The journey was dangerous, leading through a dense forest. Here they were seized by a band of armed men. It turned out that these highwaymen were all heretics embittered by the imperial decree which gave them option either to reconcile themselves to the Church or leave the country.

In danger of being killed for revenge, the priests took refuge in our Infant Jesus, promising to offer Holy Mass in His honor if their lives were spared. In confident clear voices, they had begun to chant the litany of the Holy Name of Jesus when the miracle happened. It seemed to them as if the Infant Jesus used their misfortune to manifest His power, to say again, *Ego sum*. As if struck by lightning, the bandits fled, concerned only with their personal safety. The priests went on their way unmolested, saved from the hands of would-be-murderers, thanks to the Infant Jesus.

XLI

THE INFANT SAVES ONE TEMPTED FROM ETERNAL DAMNATION

Caught by a sudden storm while they were off the shore of Genesareth, the disciples of Christ recognized their great danger. But Christ their Master lay peacefully asleep in the boat. Yet later that same Master went into the Garden of Olives accompanied by three disciples. This time the situation was reversed, the Master kept vigil, as He had done through many other nights of prayer. How can we explain the difference? Was not danger present in both instances? In the storm upon the lake, the physical well-being of his disciples was at stake; in Gethsemani, their souls were endangered by temptation. That is the reason for His warning: *Vigilate, ut non intretis in tentationem.* Watch that you shall not be tempted. It would seem that Christ sleeps, as it were, when the body only is endangered, but when a faithful soul is tempted, then He stands by, ready with His help.

Such aid He brought to a certain nobleman, whose name we prefer to conceal here out of consideration for his family. The Emperor had elevated a certain baron to a position of great importance which, for some unknown reason, he feared would be recalled from him. The thought of it hurt his pride and touched the glory of his family reputation. So depressed did he become that he had decided to take his own life. But before the opportunity came for this, God showed His mercy. Father Cyril came unexpectedly to visit and judged from the countenance of the distraught man what great crisis his soul was experiencing. He approached the man with soothing words, recalling God's great mercy and His willingness to help. Finally the man was persuaded to visit in company with Father Cyril the chapel of the Infant Jesus.

Consider the power and love of this Infant! At the sight of His image, this poor man felt so deeply moved that he wept openly and confessed his sins. After the reception of Holy Communion, in thanksgiving for being freed of his depressed state and the temptation of suicide, he put into writing the following vow:

Ex voto: I, N.N., hereby solemnly declare that I will give to the Discalced Carmelite Fathers one hundred ducats in honor of the Infant Jesus, provided I shall be delivered from the fears which haunt me and on the condition that no dishonor will befall me.
March 22, 1650.

(L.S.) N.N.

This document he laid at the feet of the Infant, and returned home in wonderful spirits. And the miracle was a lasting one: from this time on he lived free from melancholy and fear, and achieved honors in the discharge of his position. In gratitude he returned to the monastery with a donation of a hundred ducats, and the gift of a very beautiful chalice. These were followed by others as the years went on.

XLII

A PRIEST IS HEALED OF HIS HIGH FEVER

Twice in holy scripture is there mention of Christ, the Divine Physician, healing persons ill of a fever. One cure was worked in favor of the son of the royal official of Capharnaum; the other, in favor of Peter's mother-in-law. Consider the circumstances that distinguish these miraculous cures. The officer's son was close to death when his father hurried out to meet Jesus, begging Him to "come down before my child dies." St. John tells us that Jesus spoke words of comfort to the stricken father: "Go thy way, thy son lives." (John 5:48). The mother-in-law of Peter suffered from a similar ailment. Jesus, we are told, visited her and worked a miracle for her recovery. You are wondering why the Savior came in person to Peter's house, for the express purpose of healing his relative, while in the case of the official of Capharnaum, the cure was worked *in absentia,* in recognition of the official's faith. Was Peter's faith less praiseworthy than this father's?

The answer to your question lies in understanding the words of Jesus, *Petite et accipietis!* Where faith supports the request no prayer remains unanswered with God. The boy at Capharnaum lay at a distance from the place where Christ and his disciples were; to go to him personally would have delayed the apostolic work in which Christ was engaged. He might easily have healed Peter's mother-in-law in the same manner, but her case, lying in the immediate vicinity of His preaching, was handled immediately and personally in the most reasonable and appropriate way.

The Divine Physician continued to go about doing good. In 1650 Father Vitus, one of our fathers, lay desperately ill of a fever. It was a hopeless case, according to the doctor attending him. But because Vitus understood what Jesus meant by His promise, "Ask and you shall receive," he came with strong faith and perfect trust to request the Infant for recovery. If spared, he vowed to celebrate Holy Mass in the chapel of the Infant, and to recite the Litany of His Holy Name daily. The fever abated, and the monk lived to praise the divine Child for his return to health.

XLIII

A STRICKEN WOMAN IS MIRACULOUSLY CURED BY THE INFANT

Is there a man who cannot say with the psalmist

David, "I am Yours, because You have created me; I am Yours because You have saved me: I am Yours, because you have made me a Christian." Those who can say truly as David did that he is the Lord's will escape as truly as David did whatever danger threatens him.

Lady Eva Febronia Pernthal's case is to the point. This noblewoman apparently was in the best of health when she began her journey into Lojovice to visit her estates there, accompanied by her chaplains. On the night of her arrival she suffered a sudden severe heart attack, and her chaplain-confessor summoned to her bedside found her already rigid, hardly able to give a sign of life. Knowing what confidence his penitent had placed in the Infant on previous occasions, the priest recommended Lady Pernthal to entrust herself now to His loving care. His reassuring words were heard, and the unconscious patient suddenly regained her senses. In a clear and firm voice she recited the powerful prayer of Father Cyril. The following morning found her in normal health and able to discharge her domestic duties. She received the sacrament of Penance and went to Holy Communion, and in gratitude for her recovery, presented as gifts to the monastery a beautiful Turkish rug, an antependium, and liturgical vestments for Mass. She made it a custom through the years to renew her thanks with other gifts. It became her daily practice to recite the Litany of the Most Holy Name.

XLIV

DEATH COMES TO AN UNGRATEFUL CLIENT OF THE INFANT — 1650

Count the breaths you breathe, the steps you take each day. They are the natural means which bring you ever closer to the throne of Christ, your Judge, where you shall receive reward or punishment for your deeds in this life. The Lord will reward everyone according to his deeds. Our Lord frequently makes use of signs and significant examples to impress upon us this fact of judgment.

A high-ranking nobleman (whose name we withhold) took seriously ill in August, 1650, suffering from a urinary obstruction which had resulted in his present edematose condition. It appeared rather obvious that he would die unless relieved. Father Cyril, his father confessor, was called in to administer the last rites. He prepared the man for death, then counseled him in the following manner:

"Your Honor, nothing at all happens — not even a leaf falls from a tree — unknown to the will of God. 'Without Me you can do nothing,' said our Savior. I advise you, therefore, to turn to that One from Whom all blessings flow as from an eternal spring, to Jesus Christ our only salvation. As the divine Infant He is ready to bestow miracles on the devout faithful. Many have already received His wonderful gifts of grace and mercy. You can make yourself worthy of such a miracle by conforming to the recommendations already given." (And here Father Cyril outlined the method for obtaining favors that we have described elsewhere in this book.)

The patient gave close attention to Father Cyril's words. "I believe you," he said, "and want to make my confession and carry out your advice." As a sign of his goodwill he promised to give two thousand florins to the honor of the Infant, asking for relief from his ailment and the strength to write his will and settle his business affairs. Relief came quickly and the swelling in his body noticeably decreased. With tears in his eyes the patient raised his hands in thankful prayer. So does the Lord reward the good. But as He is also just, He has to deal with the wicked, meting out punishment for evil.

This man, once he had regained his health, set about making good his promise. Unfortunately, however, he persuaded his wife to assume the responsibility of paying the promised money to the monastery. This the avaricious woman failed to do, making all kinds of excuses for putting off payment of the debt. But she suffered punishment for this neglect; her husband died suddenly without having left a will, thus depriving her of the large inheritance she had expected. This incident recalls the fact of the last judgment, where God in His wisdom will reward the good and punish the evil.

XLV

THE PEOPLE OF SOLNICE ARE CONVERTED THROUGH DEVOTION TO THE INFANT

On one occasion our blessed Savior ordered His disciples to throw out the fishing net over the right side of their boat, and as a result of their obedience they had difficulty pulling in the catch, so plentiful was it. There would appear to be some mystery here, until we recall that St. Jerome assigns the number one hundred and fifty-three to the number of species of fish. The fisherman's net in the parable is the symbol of the preaching of the gospel. In their mission, then, the apostles had caught the whole world. Centuries before, the Prophet Habacuc had prophesied: "And thou wilt make men as the fishes of the sea. . . . He lifted up all of them with his hook, he drew them in his drag and gathered them into it; for this He will be glad and rejoice." (Habacuc 1:14). Again the Lord threw out the net, so to speak; this time, through our priests in an effort to convert the inhabitants of Solnice.

For twenty years, in spite of imperial decrees and threats of punishment these people had stubbornly clung to their heretical beliefs. In 1650 our Prior added their conversion to his many other obligations. For this cause so close to his heart, he ordered Holy Mass to be offered at the chapel of the Infant each day until his return from Solnice. In his company came three priests well versed in the Czech language. The missioners made public the reason of their coming, but the people of Solnice, incited to riot by certain fanatics among them, threatened their very lives. There seemed little hope of succeeding in the task of conversion.

The missioners continued to preach the gospel of the Catholic faith, and to report the many miracles performed by God through intercession of the holy Infant of Prague. In July, 1647, the Carmelite Fathers had set up in the parish church of Solnice a replica of the image of the Infant, made of wood and touched to the original one in Prague. Finally the stubborn hearts of the people were touched, and they agreed to give up their heresy, and accept the true faith. In large numbers they made their confessions, and after instructions and public profession of the Catholic faith, they received Holy Communion. This miracle of the people of Solnice's return to the true faith must be credited to the Infant Jesus. May His name be blessed forever!

XLVI

INGRATITUDE AND INCONSTANCY IN PRAYER ARE PUNISHED — 1650

Toward Saul, the enemy who sought to kill him, David showed merciful forgiveness. But toward Nabal, likewise his enemy, he showed great anger, even to taking up arms to revenge himself. Human beings become enraged as Nabal did when they receive ingratitude for kindnesses. Likewise the

Lord must be angered at the lack of gratitude on the part of men despite His benevolence toward them. What good is it to cultivate the field in spring, and let the summer pass by, the crop unreaped? What good for the vineyard to stand heavy with blossom, its vines laden with fruit, if hail comes to destroy the harvest? Therefore will the Lord punish those persons whose so-called devotion does not stem from a sincere heart. Such an example of inconstancy we set forth in the previous chapter. There are many cases which demonstrate this matter of ingratitude, these two among others:

A certain Baroness had received benevolent graces from the Infant Jesus. But she fell off in her expressions of gratitude, her devotions becoming less frequent and her prayer less sincere. The matter went even farther than this. In imitation of the image at Prague, she had a replica made, which she claimed as powerful as the image in the monastery. Noticeably less devout herself she soon exercised an influence in this direction over others. But see now how our loving Infant showed His dissatisfaction with such inconstancy! Within a short time both her husband and eldest son died. A younger son who had taken on part of his father's business was afflicted with apoplexy, lost the faculty of speech, and never regained the mental health he had lost during his illness. Silver and gold, valued at many thousand gulden, were stolen from her house in Prague, and the house itself burned at the hands of the thieves. By falsifying a statement she incurred the displeasure of the Emperor, was liable to a fine of several thousand gulden, and suffered the loss of her reputation. But in these severe punishments, the Baroness was able to discover the hand of God, and regretting her infidelity to grace, renewed her devotions to the Infant.

A similar case was this: a noblewoman had to endure hardships that followed after she forsook the Infant. Her husband was taken prisoner of war, and her worldly possessions seized by enemy vandals. She tried without success to raise the money to ransom him. Her failure depressed her, and her move to divorce him scandalized the society in which she moved. Formerly regarded as a devout and pious person she was looked upon with suspicion, and charged with being irresponsible. Driven by this fact to attempt suicide, she was saved when the Infant Jesus, because of her precious devotion to Him, intervened. She saw the malice of her sin and sought forgiveness. She resumed her devotion to the Infant, and promised to say in His honor every day the litany of the Most Holy Name.

XLVII

THE PRIOR IS REPROVED FOR HIS RELAXED DEVOTION — 1651

Numquid oblivisci potest mulier infantum suum, ut non misereatur filii uteri sui? Is it possible, the prophet Isaias asks us, that a mother forsake her own child, that she show no mercy toward the son of her womb? Is it possible she will leave him unprovided? Even so, I will not forsake you. I will be more than a mother to you.

But what is the reason for these words of eternal mercy spoken by the prophet to the children of God? If a child falls to the floor his mother will lift him up; she will make him neat and clean if he has become soiled; bring him food and drink if he is in need of these; protect him in time of danger. If he insults her and begs forgiveness for the insults, she will forgive the child, taking him into her arms. All these things the mother does to make her child grow in goodness. She loves him too much to desert him in his need. However truly great a mother's love is, that of the Infant Jesus is still greater.

It was a filial kind of love our Prior manifested towards the Infant, the love of a child towards his mother. He urged others to feel the same kind of affection, inspiring them to worship him publicly. But gradually the Prior began to relax his personal devotion. When consulted about permission to enlarge the chapel — something which could have been done without great expenditure of money — he refused that permission, explaining that he needed money to build and furnish an infirmary in the monastery. But shortly afterwards, he had no explanation for the fact that the building fund put into a safe seemed to have vanished! This he felt to be a great discredit to himself, a punishment for having started to build what he was not able to finish.

The Prior then gave his permission for the building plans, realizing the wrong he had done by withholding his approval. The Infant Jesus, always as loving and solicitous as a mother to her child, sent benefactors to the monastery with gifts amounting to two hundred florins.

But how inconstant at times are we poor human beings! The Prior indeed recognized the hand of the Infant Jesus in these benefactions, and rejoiced at them. But again he postponed the chapel project, holding there was greater need for an infirmary. This he did out of love for his neighbor, but he himself was to suffer the folly of his decision. Taken violently ill, he could find no relief at all until he had approved the use of fifty florins for the remodeling of the chapel. Like a gracious mother, the Infant recognized his decision by granting him an immediate recovery.

Unfortunately there was still not sufficient money to carry out construction. The Prior was approached again, this time to ask if two of the monastery carpenters could assist with the task, in this way reducing the costs. This request he refused, in order to exercise the patience of his subordinates, but was again personally to suffer for the delay. When his health took a sudden relapse into his previous serious condition, he came finally to realize that he was being reproved for such conduct by the Infant. He was completely well by the time the chapel addition was erected. This expense was taken care of by several benefactors whose combined gifts totaled two thousand five hundred and nine florins. Blessed be the gracious Infant for this generosity!

XLVIII

THE COUNTS OF MARTINIC EXPERIENCE THE MERCIES OF THE INFANT — 1651

Domine, quem amas infirmatur. Lord, the one whom You love is sick. This was the message Martha and Mary sent by messenger to Christ, reporting the illness of their brother Lazarus. Why did the sisters not go themselves in person? There was a distance of only two miles separating them from the Master. Jairus and the royal official of Capharnaum, as the gospel narratives relate, made their requests of Christ personally, asking a miraculous cure for their loved ones. Perhaps it is because these sisters of Lazarus are very certain of the great love Christ bore their brother. "Lord, the one You love is ill." And this was enough. Love never waits to be asked; it stands by, ever ready to help, seeking opportunities to give more than the need demands.

This special love and many untold graces of the Infant Jesus were the experience of the Martinic family.

His Excellency, Count Adam Martinic, took critically ill in 1651. He resided in Vienna that year, filling the post of High Chancellor. Physicians gave no hope of his recovery. Benna Martinic, Provost of Vysehrad, the Count's brother, hastened to his bedside, promising before he left for Vienna to donate twenty ducats to the monastery for his brother's return to health. This vow he put into writing, reminding the Infant Jesus that "one whom You love is sick." *Vade, frater tuus vivit.* Go, your brother lives. At the same hour that the promise was made and prayer offered before the image of the Infant Jesus, word came with news of the sick man's recovery.

On November 21, 1649, His Excellency, Count Jaroslav Martinic, passed to his eternal reward. Bernard Ignatius had reason to believe that the Martinic family would no longer continue to fill the post of High Chancellor of Bohemia which his late father held, because Ferdinand IV, as king of Bohemia, had announced his intention of residing in Prague. He therefore posted a letter to our Fathers in Prague, asking for counsel and prayers. A favorable answer came through a decree of the Emperor, who turned the office over to the Count. He succeeded to his father's position on January 14, a date he chose in honor of the beloved Infant, the feast day of the Most Holy Name of Jesus. Installed as Supreme Burgrave of the Kingdom, he came in person to our monastery and paid public veneration to the image, leaving an offering as *ex voto.*

It was not long, however, until Count Bernard Martinic fell ill. To prevent further complications in his case, his doctors ordered complete relaxation and a leave of absence from his official duties. The Chancellor doubted the Emperor would grant such a permission so short a time after his installation in office, but he hurried to the Infant with the petition, "Lord, the one You love is ill." Again, and with wonderful love the Infant responded. The desired permission was obtained, and the prescribed rest brought the Count complete recovery. The expression of Bernard Martinic's gratitude was a beautiful gold and silver jewel-studded crown for the image of the Infant King.

XLIX

FOR THE FIRST TIME THE FEAST OF THE INFANT IS SOLEMNLY CELEBRATED — 1651

All Christians celebrate January 6, the Feast of the Epiphany, as the public manifestation of the Divine Child to the Magi, the first ones to recognize His kingship in a public way. *Ubi est, qui natus est Rex?* they asked. And they worshipped Him, paying the tribute due a king. Now perhaps we understand why the Invitatory (meaning the invitation to adore) is omitted from Matins prescribed for this day. It is in commemoration of the readiness of the Wise Men; they did not wait for an invitation. Once they saw His star, they set out bearing gifts.

The ceremony held on January 14, 1651, was especially festive. The image of the King of kings, the gracious Infant of Prague, was carried in solemn procession from his chapel home in the monastery to the church. There in a tabernacle, where otherwise only the Blessed Sacrament is exposed, the holy image was placed, and a joyous chant sung in honor of the Most Holy Name.

This was the day on which the nobility of Prague gathered to proclaim him their King. They brought Him precious gifts, tokens of gratitude for the liberation of Prague during its recent siege. On this day He was crowned with the title "Infant Jesus, full of grace." The noblemen present were like the kings of old: ready to come at the first invitation of the monks to attend the royal feast in person. It is our duty—and our honor—to mention among the noblemen present: Count Bernard Ignatius Martinic, Supreme Burgrave, Prince Lichtenstein and his wife, Countess Galla, Count Philip von Mansfeld, Count von Nestice, Supreme County Judge, Count Kolowrat, President of the Chamber.

The Feast of the Infant Jesus was celebrated in this fashion every succeeding year as long as our Reverend Archbishop and our honorable Chancellor lived. Their example of devoted allegiance to the little Infant Jesus was an inspiration to the whole aristocracy.

L

THE SERIOUSLY ILL ARE CURED BY THE INFANT

Is it not strange that Christ hesitated to grant the petition of the woman of Canaan? Was not her prayer for her daughter's cure made humbly, on her knees before the Master? "It is not right to take the bread of the children and cast it to the dogs," was Christ's answer to his disciples' plea in her behalf. Why does He hesitate to use His power of healing on this Canaanite when, as St. Luke expresses it, He "radiates strength." Christ does all things to teach us a lesson. Here it is the lesson to persevere in prayer, if no answer is forthcoming at once; or if what we pray for is denied, to accept it as the will of God working for our salvation of soul. God's love is enormous, and if what we ask for is for the good of our soul and we pray for it with lively faith and a firm hope, He will surely grant our request. This is proved by numerous miracles granted through the Infant during the year 1651.

Prince Ferdinand John Lichtenstein's colitis grew so acute that it threatened his life. As the pain grew more intense, there appeared the danger of death. In this crisis he turned to the Infant, promising a personal visit to His chapel and reception of Penance and Holy Communion. His prayers were answered, and he fulfilled his promise gratefully.

Mrs. Catherine Wendlinger grew extremely ill with consumption, the type that doctors claimed was incurable. But she likewise turned for a cure from the divine Physician, the Infant Jesus, promising to confess and receive Holy Communion. In gratitude for her cure, she burned votive candles before the holy image.

An undiagnosed disease was threatening the life of John Ernest Tyralla, Imperial Registrar. Medical treatments seemed only to aggravate his condition. He refused further medicine and begged the Infant to restore his health, promising to contribute something to the chapel. His recovery was complete, and in fulfillment of his vow, he had made several cabinets for use in the chapel.

In military service, on his way to Maria Loretto, Lady Kropp's son became so ill his company had to leave him behind in the care of strangers. His mother worried over his welfare, promising to give some token of gratitude if her only son were spared to return home. In answer to prayer her son recovered, rejoined his company and returned to Prague, where his grateful mother gave an offering of nine florins and several yards of gold fringe to be used for decorative purposes on the altar of the Infant.

LI

A DIFFICULT CONFINEMENT IS RECOMMENDED TO THE INFANT — 1652

Egenus et pauper sum ego. In no sense was he a pauper, yet King David counted himself miserably poor. I am miserable and poor. Why do the rich as well as the poor claim themselves miserable? True, the day dawns equally soon and as surely for both the rich and the poor. But with some persons, there comes with the day this worry: how can I get through the day; where may I find my daily bread? Here then is the difference. Where the poor man places his faith in God and His provident love, the rich trust in their earthly goods and human help. *Iste pauper clamavit, et Dominus exaudivit eum. Desiderium pauperum exaudivit Dominus.* David wished to emphasize that he had not placed his trust and faith in worldly things and men; that his only hope was God. For this reason he called himself a pauper, and God heard his cry for help.

Maria Tyralla's life was endangered after she had given birth to her child. The case baffled her doctor, and human aid seemed helpless in her case. Father Cyril, the woman's confessor, counseled her to place her welfare into the hands of the Infant. She became strong and well again, fulfilling David's promise that the poor desiring God's help will be objects of His loving care. In return Mrs. Tyralla made a sacrifice of something very dear to her, and promised a Holy Mass each week in honor of the Infant.

LII

THE INFANT JESUS IS PEACE-MAKER IN DOMESTIC AFFAIRS — 1652

There is mystery for us in the story of the miracle at Cana. Why, if our Lord wished to produce wine by a miracle, did He not simply will that the pitchers be filled with wine immediately? Why did He fill the vessels first with water? First of all, understand that the water pitcher at the wedding feast symbolizes the heart of two persons. The warming wine stands for their united love; but water, from the very beginning, was a divided thing. Therefore it symbolizes disunion. It is as though Christ said: "I will change water into wine; I will change disunity or hostility in the hearts of this couple into love and peaceful unity." The symbolism of the wedding in Cana can be transformed into reality through the Infant, as the following story indicates.

A certain noblewoman suffered greatly from her husband's jealousy. Things had gone so far that no one expected a reconciliation; the jealous partner had already threatened the wife with death. Her father confessor counseled the innocent wife to bring her distress of mind to the Prince of Peace, the Infant Jesus. This she did, with the promise of a testimonial of gratitude. Miraculously, marital peace was restored, and she and her husband lived henceforth in love and harmony. Both offered to thank the Infant by generous gifts.

LIII

AN ARISTOCRAT IS SAVED FROM IMPRISONMENT — 1652

You recall the accusations made against the innocent Susanna by two ancients of the people who were the appointed judges for that year. Condemned to die on a false charge of adultery, how did this innocent woman conduct herself? Did she speak out in her own defense? No, for she realized how useless that would be. Instead she sent up her sighs to God in prayer, pouring out her heart to Him in Whom alone she trusted. And behold what good came of her trust! "The Lord raised up the spirit of a young boy, Daniel" who convicted her accusers of false witness. (Dan. 13:45)

A perversion of justice once threatened the life of an accused aristocrat. An officer of the imperial army had been entrusted by fellow officers with a thousand florins. After the Swedish invasion he was so desperately in need of money that he presumed to borrow these funds entrusted to him for safekeeping, never doubting his ability to replace them. But when he least expected it, the officers demanded their savings, and because he could not produce them, demanded his imprisonment. His own defense went unheeded. In this extremity he turned to the Infant, promising frequent Confession and Holy Communion and daily recitation of the Litany of the Most Holy Name and the prayer given in the preface. (Father Cyril's prayer.) Three days later his debtors came, offering to settle peacefully. Released from prison, the officer's first act was to visit the chapel of the Infant to express his gratitude.

LIV

THE OWNERSHIP OF SOLNICE IS SECURED THROUGH THE INFANT — 1652

The giant Goliath went before Saul and said: "Choose out a man of you, and let him come down and fight hand to hand. If he be able to fight with me and kill me, we will be servants to you; but if I prevail against him, and kill him, you shall be servants." (I Kings 17:6) This kind of talk from their Philistine enemy frightened the Israelites, for none of the warriors was willing to meet the giant under this condition. But then came the boy David, "ruddy and of a comely countenance," who volunteered for the combat and killed the giant single-handed with a stone from a sling. By this act he secured victory for the Israelites over their enemy, and peace for his people.

The Carmelite estate in Solnice was threatened when a claimant, Count Magni, brought suit against the monks, disputing their rights to the property. Actually his claim was very slight, but he had many friends who brought their influence to bear upon the case, until it was feared the estates in Solnice were about to be registered in Magni's name. The monks lacked an advocate for their cause, except the Infant Jesus, before Whose image the monks prayed fervently. On the day when the transfer of deed was to be effected, word came that Count Magni had taken suddenly ill, and without regaining consciousness, he died the following day. This was not the first time that litigation concerning the ownership of Solnice had arisen, but each time the Infant Jesus protected the rights of the Order, and finally proper registration was made in the Office of Land Registry, acknowledging the Carmelites as the legal owners.

LV

THOSE WHO DISGRACE THE INFANT ARE PUNISHED — 1652-1653

Consider what happened as news of the birth of Jesus reached King Herod. Whereas the three kings were overjoyed at the news, Herod was overcome with fear and envy. The former followed the star and came to worship the new-born King; the latter sought to kill Him. To those who worship Him, God never fails to show His mercy; to those who dishonor His name, He metes out punishment.

In 1652 the miraculous favors bestowed through the Infant had attracted widespread praise. But one person was heard to say mockingly: What do I care about the Infant Jesus at the Discalced Carmel? There are images in other churches where such miracles could be performed! For his abusive words he was punished, suffering a severe rupture.

The same year our sacristan tried to have the celebration of Holy Mass transferred to the church. Possibly he did this from a worthy motive, but it meant that veneration of the holy image would be taken out of the chapel of the Infant. The change lasted only one day — the feast of the Holy Trinity — but it displeased the Infant very much. The sacristan, a strong and healthy man until now, was afflicted with gout so painful that he became bed-ridden.

Such was the punishment of those who dishonored the Infant. But the reverse is true of those who venerated Him faithfully, as this incident of 1653 will show. A certain priest tried to lift too heavy an object, and in doing so badly ruptured himself. Hesitating to speak of his condition to others, he asked permission of his superior to visit the Infant at the Discalced Carmelite monastery. Prostrate at the feet of the image, he prayed to be delivered from his infirmity, promising if cured to recite daily the Litany of the Holy Name. He left the chapel without any of the crippling pain with which he had come there, and suffered no further evidence of his former trouble.

The same year Rudolphus von Friessleben was prepared for death. He had suffered a long illness without hope of recovery. But after promising the Infant to visit His chapel and receive the sacraments, he began noticeably to improve in health. In gratitude he burned six candles before the image.

LVI

A BISHOPRIC IS FILLED THROUGH THE INFANT

In what manner did Peter receive the highest post in the government of the Church? *Tu es Christus Filius Dei vivi,* was his profession of faith in the divinity of Christ. And Christ had responded: *Tu es Petrus et super hanc petram ædificabo Ecclesiam meam. Et tibi dabo claves regni coelorum.* (Thou art Peter, and upon this rock I will build my church and I will give thee the keys of the kingdom of heaven.) Thus you answer, Peter received his post because of his profession of belief in the divinity of Christ. But I hold that it was not so much for *faith* as for his love of Christ that he was rewarded. Peter was asked three times to declare his love: "Lovest thou Me more than these?" And three times he made answer, "Lord, Thou knowest that I love Thee." Then it was that the Lord appointed him Prince of the Church, and Pastor to lead His sheep to the pasture of truth. *Pasce oves meas; pasce agnes meos.* From this incident it might be rightly concluded that love for God is a requisite condition for the honor of bishop.

When the Right Reverend Crispini, Prelate of Strahov and Suffragan bishop of Prague, passed away on August 23, 1653, there were many who sought the episcopal office he held. One of these, a special protegé of the Emperor and a man sponsored by His Eminence, the Cardinal Archbishop of Prague, seemed certain to be named to the office. But the Reverend Joseph de Corte, who had been first steward to the Cardinal for many years, also aspired to this office. He celebrated Holy Mass one day before the image in our monastery for this intention, pledging his devotion to the Holy Infant if he were to attain the desired honor. For some reason never made known, the likely candidate was dropped, and within a few days Father Joseph de Corte received word of his appointment. He was consecrated the following September as Archbishop of Sebaste. He counted this unusual grace a manifestation of God's will through the Infant, and was grateful for it during the remainder of his life.

LVII

AN ARISTOCRAT COUPLE ARE BLESSED WITH A MALE HEIR

It was the hour for offering incense in the temple. Zachary, the high priest, was at prayer in the temple of the Lord when an angel appeared and said: "Zachary, your prayers have been granted; your wife will be delivered of a son." Considering that Zachary's prayers were for his people, with no thought about a son (for he was old and his wife barren) this message is puzzling. Why does the angel promise him an answer to prayers for a son? Because the Lord is generous, and sometimes gives unasked even those things which seem unobtainable to human endeavor.

For many years, the marriage of the nobleman, Christopher Ferdinand, Baron of Lobkowitz, and his wife remained unblessed by children. He made frequent trips to the chapel of the Infant, begging God to grant them a son. The Infant heard the prayers, and the Lobkowitz family rejoiced over the birth of their only son within the year. On his birthday, December 14, 1654, the Baron expressed his gratitude with the gift of three thousand florins for the use of the Carmelite monastery.

LVIII

A WOMAN'S LIFE IS SPARED AND MENTAL HEALTH RESTORED TO HER SON — 1655

David once suffered bitterly, we are told, from a lack of warmth. Was this because of insufficient clothing? No; a king has no dearth of clothing to keep his body comfortably clad. Clothes alone are not the sole source of heat; the body must furnish its own warmth. Clothe a statue of Saul, or a corpse, and neither will be warmed thereby. The reason, then, why David suffered is that he had lost his interior heat. Where that state prevails, no amount of exterior covering will produce the needed warmth. So it is with prayer; no matter how lengthy, we will find our prayer to be in vain if we feel not the heat of God's love. But even the shortest prayer animated with the fire of the love of God will penetrate the heavens and move Him to grant an answer. Remember the cry of Peter on the water, "Lord, save me!" (Matt. 14:30) It was a short but fervent cry for help, and Peter and his companions were saved from the fury of the waves.

The only son of the pious Mrs. Kropp suffered a brain damage that affected his mind. Confused and in great pain he one day threatened his mother's life with a loaded gun. The terrified woman sent up an agonized plea to the Infant, Whom she dearly loved. "O Infant Jesus, have mercy on me!" The son fired, but the bullet missed its mark. After her miraculous escape from death, she tried in every way to help restore her son to mental health. Even after a long series of treatments which brought no apparent improvement in his condition, she did not despair. When her prayers to the Infant at last brought complete recovery, she rejoiced at the miracles and demonstrated her gratitude in every possible way.

LIX

THE INFANT JESUS IS CROWNED PUBLICLY — 1655

The history of the Old Testament brings to light the wisdom of God in the matter of the ceremony in which an earthly king receives his crown. The place prescribed is always near a well or within the shade of a tree. The symbolism is this: only he is worthy of the kingly crown who, like a well, will provide refreshing water to the thirsty, or like a tree, will share his fruit with the hungry among his people.

We have mentioned numerous occasions when our monastery was favored: how richly the Infant rewarded the prayers of those who came there in need; how often the sorrowful were made glad, the sick restored to health and dangers averted. It would seem the fitting thing, therefore, to express a demonstration of gratefulness by means of a public coronation ceremony.

His Excellency, Count Bernard Martinic, Burgrave of the Kingdom of Bohemia, visited the chapel of the Infant on the occasion of his annual retreat at our monastery. It was his custom at the close of these days of quiet prayer and private worship to donate a rich gift. In 1654 his special Christmas offering was a royal crown studded with precious jewels. April 4 was selected as the date for the solemn coronation, to which the whole aristocracy of Prague were invited. Because of the illness that prevented the Cardinal Archbishop from presiding, this honor fell to the Archbishop of Sebaste, Joseph de Corte. Clad in episcopal robes, His Excellency celebrated Holy Mass in the chapel beautifully adorned for the occasion. After the Offertory prayers, he placed the crown upon the head of the beloved image, then proceeded to the end of the Holy Sacrifice. After Mass he knelt in adoration and kissed the feet of the Infant as a symbol of allegiance; all the noblemen including the Burgrave followed his example. Count Martinic himself asked for the special favor of being named to the Order of the Golden Fleece by His Spanish Majesty. When this honor was later granted, he ordered a replica of this insignia made for the Infant, and he himself placed it as an expression of thanksgiving.

LX

THE INFANT IS TRANSFERRED TO THE CHURCH FOR PUBLIC VENERATION

Those who thoughtfully read the history of the Holy Image are struck with the similarity it bears to the history of the Ark of the Covenant built by Moses at the command of God. This Old Testament Ark of the Lord stood between two adoring cherubims. It had no permanent place, but for years was moved around. To some of the faithful Israelites, God granted mercy under this Ark; to others His justice meted out punishment. So it is with the throne of our living Ark, the Infant Jesus. *Ipse est propitiatio pro peccatis nostris.* He is the propitiation for our sins, says St. John. Like the Ark of the Lord, the Holy Image has found a permanent home in the church of God. He has been taken out of his hidden chapel where veneration was restricted to certain persons into a place of worship, where all may come to venerate.

On March 19, 1656, the Infant was carried in solemn procession by Carmelite monks, attired in their monastic cloaks and carrying lighted candles, into the new shrine. The new place of worship was the gift of John Ernest and Francis William Talmberg. They were inspired to honor the Infant in this way from the example of their cousin, Baron John Talmberg, who had built a similar chapel in the same church in honor of Our Lady of Mount Carmel. Like him they also offered twenty-five hundred florins in Mass stipends. This chapel was consecrated on July 16, 1655, the first Mass being celebrated there by Auxiliary Archbishop De Corte.

ANNOTATION

One might assume that once the image of the Infant had been brought out of hiding, as it were, and set up in the church for public veneration that the wonders He had already worked would henceforth be multiplied. But on the contrary, the next few years were quiet ones in the history of the image. I cannot offer any explanation for this. I cannot help recalling, however, the words the Infant once spoke to our Father Cyril, as mentioned previously. "As you honor Me, so will I reward you." Could it be that here, exposed for public veneration, the Infant was the recipient of less honor than in His retirement in the monastery chapel? *Quod rarum, carum.* The rarer they are, the more highly are things esteemed. We should not wonder why; the once profuse miracles of the Infant were now more sparingly bestowed because of a decreased devotion.

LXI

THE FAMILY OF THE COUNTS VON SCHLICK RECEIVE SPECIAL GRACES — 1656-1665

Note the braggadocio of Zacchaeus as he told Christ, "Behold, Lord, I give half of my possessions to the poor, and if I have defrauded anyone of anything I restore it fourfold." (Luke 19:8) But for all this boasting, Jesus said to him, "Today salvation has come to this house." Not so did He bless the Pharisee who also boasted: "I fast twice a week; I pay tithes of all that I possess." (Luke 18:12) The difference lies in the motives by which these two men were moved. God looks into the hearts of men. If he finds there a lack of goodness, the deed that comes from that heart has no value in His eyes. The boastful Pharisee was praising no one but himself, and the Lord was not pleased; the publican Zacchaeus had for his purpose the honor of God. Therefore was it said of him: *Salus huic domui facta est.*

I do not purpose to list in detail all the benefits our monastery received through the generosity of the Counts of Schlick, nor mention all the favors this family received through devotion to the Infant Jesus. But I do wish to describe how, because of their devotion, the Infant blessed this house.

Countess Margareta Schlick became dangerously ill in 1656. Because she was pregnant at the time, it was feared that neither mother nor child would live. But her fervent prayers to the Infant were answered favorably, and she survived the dangerous childbirth. In gratitude for a safe delivery the Countess brought a gift of two silver candelabra to adorn the altar of the new chapel on March 19, the day the image was transferred to its new place of veneration.

Count Francis Ernest Schlick suffered from gout and a kidney disorder that the doctors had at first wrongly diagnosed as intestinal trouble. The condition became so serious he prepared for death, sending an offering of sixty florins to the monastery with a request for prayers. When Father Cyril paid the Count a visit, he heard of the great confidence the sick man placed in the Infant. He received the latter's promise that if spared, he would provide a permanent trust to propagate the work of the foundation, set up in 1650 to honor the Infant by a weekly Mass. His promise made, almost immediately the Count felt some relief of his painful affliction. There was no further need for medical treatment and in a short time he had completely recovered his health.

LXII

A POSSESSED PERSON IS RELIEVED OF A DEVIL BEFORE THE IMAGE — 1664

There is a moral to draw from the story of the demoniac cured by Christ. As soon as the man so afflicted was brought into Christ's presence he called out, "Jesus, son of the Most High, do not hurt me!" It would seem that the demon was forced to confess, "O Jesus, I cannot exist in Your presence; allow me to flee quickly." Does it not seem strange that the devil should suddenly desire to quit a body he had so long inhabited? And, why, too, did Jesus appear slow to exorcise this devil? Certainly the devil took his possession of the man swiftly and did much damage. Christ, on the other hand, came slowly, bringing him salvation.

There are two lessons in this incident. First, know that evil enters the soul in a flash, and to rid oneself of evil is a difficult and time-consuming task. A second lesson: in the presence of Jesus, evil cannot endure. Recall that upon His entrance as an Infant into the land of Egypt, the idols there collapsed, allowing the evil spirits therein to escape. A case of exorcism from the power of evil can be recalled here:

Maria Fremmin, a native of Kaysers-Berg in Silesia, cursed it was said by a sorceress, was sent by a priest from Litomerice to seek a cure in Prague when all means of exorcism in her native Silesia had been tried in vain. Her case had first to be established as a real case of possession, not a deception induced by hysteria or other natural cause. After examination the woman was referred for exorcism to Father Cyril. In obedience to his Prior, the monk performed the mortifications and said the prayers required for this rite. He began the exorcism in the presence of the image of the Infant, first reciting the Litany of the Most Holy Name of Jesus. The cure was not effective instantly, but the woman was relieved. The devils left her one by one, and with the departure of the last, she experienced a miracle of recovery and help she had sought in vain from other sources. No doubt some persons are living yet whose parents can testify to this story of Maria Fremmin. As I sit writing this story in June, 1737, I remember an honorable old gentleman who, on a visit here to the monastery, told the monks how his own father had been an eye-witness to just such an exorcism, where the devil was cast out of a person possessed, here in the chapel of the Infant Jesus.

LXIII

THE INFANT JESUS PREVENTS AN ATTEMPTED THEFT

Frequently it has happened that persons about to commit crime are deterred by the thought of a personal injury to Jesus. They hear Him speak thus: "I am Jesus Whom you insult. I am Jesus Whose law you are treating with such contempt. I am Jesus Whose love and kindness you reward with perfidy. I am Jesus Whom you have rejected by your sins of the past." Saul heard similar words when he set out to round up the Christians for persecution and death. To this man about to execute this crime against His Holy Person, the Lord Jesus Christ identified Himself with just these words, *"Ego sum Jesus, quem tu persequeris.* I am Jesus Whom you are persecuting." (Acts 9:5) The shock of these words so affected Saul that he fell from his horse, trembling. Confessing his sin, a contrite Saul became the zealous apostle known thenceforth as Paul.

The records of 1702 provide a remarkable parallel in the case of an official (whose name we omit here in deference to his family). Guilty of planning the theft of jewels adorning the image of the Infant, this man was in the very act of removing the gold cross suspended in front when he suddenly became rigid with fear. He confessed afterwards to hearing the words, "I am Jesus, Whom you are persecuting." Ashamed of his attempted theft and resolving that no such thing would happen in the future, the would-be thief was relieved of his paralysis and left the church, repentant. But the Lord dispenses justice along with His mercies. For his intended sacrilege this man was punished. For days after, he lay critically ill, apparently near death yet unable to die. Only after he confessed his sin, and asked that his experience be made public did the soul depart, at peace with God.

LXIV

A DEVOTEE IS CURED OF PLAGUE: A SLANDERER CONTRACTS THE DISEASE

In one of their battles with the Philistines, the Israelites had already lost four thousand men, yet they were not without hope of victory. This hope they expressed by bringing into their camp the holy Ark of the Covenant. Again they engaged in combat and again they lost, this time with thirty thousand slain or wounded on the battlefield. What explanation can be offered for this, in view of the fact that the Israelites were the faithful friends of God, whereas their enemy the Philistines, the victors, were idolatrous unbelievers? Yet when the Philistine leaders heard that the holy Arks had been carried into the Israelite camp, they asked, in wonder: "Who will save us from the hand of these high gods? These are the gods who punished the Egyptians by sending them plagues!" Their praise did not go unrewarded, as we judge by their victory. The Israelites, it is true, possessed the Arks, and were confident and hopeful in their presence, yet this did not deter them from offending the divine Lawgiver. And because of this conduct, the Lord was offended, and allowed them to suffer defeat by way of punishment. Such happenings are not confined to biblical times; they occur in our own days also.

As we have shown, Prague was the scene of much suffering due to the great plague of 1713. Thousands died victim of the disease. The terrified townspeople crowded the doors of the church at dawn, beseeching the Infant to spare their lives, and their trust did not go unrewarded. One of the group, however, contracted the disease. Aware of his condition but still confident of the Infant's protection, the man took medication to break the fever and induce sweating. The following morning he got up, miraculously free of every symptom of the disease. His bedlinen and nightclothes, however, showed signs of discoloration from body poisons removed during his sleep. Overjoyed to be alive and well, the man spread the good news to all his neighbors, giving the credit for his sudden cure to the Infant. One of them, however, discredited the story, deriding the idea of a miracle. This poor woman contracted the plague herself, and died a miserable death, a warning to others — unfortunate herself not to have learned a lesson from the good fortune of another.

LXV

THE INFANT RECEIVES SPECIAL GIFTS FROM GRATEFUL CLIENTS

Divine wrath at last had hurled its thunderbolts down upon the wicked world. But through it all, Noah and his family, gathered with him in the ark, remained as safe upon angry waters as they would have been on land, sheltered by the limbs of laurels. Divine Providence had directed him here to the safety of the ark, and he felt grateful to be singled out for preservation. In recognition of the debt he owed Almighty God, Noah performed a sacrificial rite of thanksgiving. And so acceptable was Noah's thank offering, Moses informs us, that his sacrifice ascended like a sweet odor to the Lord. (Gen. 9:20) The example of Noah serves to teach us how pleasing is a grateful heart to God, who returns man's gratitude with multiplied graces.

Can we not compare this biblical flood with the great plague that afflicted Prague? There was a fearful toll in misery and death, and thousands of mourners were terrified by the danger of becoming victims. That misery we described in a previous chapter. The Infant proved Himself a living Ark to a devout neighborhood that stormed the shrine where His mercy was locked away, and received the answer of their prayers for preservation. These people, too, had good reason to recognize the debt they owed to God's loving protection of them. With grateful hearts they brought varied forms of offerings to the feet of the Infant.

One of the first to do so was Anna Clara Loragin, whose life had been spared during a critical illness. She asked for the privilege of fashioning garments for the image, in colors prescribed for liturgical feasts. Besides these and other personal gifts, she set aside the sum of a thousand, four hundred and fifty-six florins in her last will to be used to furnish the chapel with a large silver chandelier; another three hundred and ninety-nine florins she stipulated for bolts of damask; five hundred, to keep a perpetual vigil light burning; and a thousand, three hundred florins for a monstrance, inscribed to commemorate the veneration of the image, for the first time, in a place heretofore reserved exclusively for exposition of the Blessed Sacrament.

The Infant continued to be our monastery's greatest Benefactor and Provider. He had preserved us from the ravages of the plague and supplied us with the funds needed to administer many charities during that time. In thanksgiving we prepared to erect a new altar in His honor, and ornament His chapel in a more suitable manner. The funds for this renovation were furnished largely from a bequest of Maria Sybil Scheyermann, who, by will, left us the sum of fifty-nine florins as an expression of gratitude for many favors received.

Truly what Moses wrote of the sacrifice of Noah can by analogy be applied to the many donations received of benefactors: *Odoratus est Dominus odorem suavitatis.* Their lovely fragrance is a symbol of His pleasure — to be rewarded undoubtedly with eternal gifts.

LXVI

THE INFANT HEALS A BADLY INJURED HAND — 1732

Consider three remarkable things about the man healed of a withered hand as narrated by the evangelist. Unasked to perform this miracle, Christ chose the Sabbath on which to do so. Why? "Stretch forth your hand," he invited the sick man. (Mark 3:5) This gesture was not at all necessary; our Lord could most certainly have healed without it. The answer may be summarized thus: Jesus healed the man with the withered hand on a day consecrated to the honor of God to remind us all to be especially generous with offerings to Him on holy days. He effected the cure without being requested — something He is always ready to do where there is need. And the outstretched hand of the sick man is a symbol of His own hand extended in loving care to heal all manner of physical and spiritual ills afflicting mankind.

John George Achbauer, an outstanding Christian gentleman famed for his skill as an architect, was also well-known as a benefactor of the Infant. In September, 1732, he met with an accident that resulted in a dislocation in his hand. Improper treatment aggravated the condition, causing him severe pain for several months. It was decided finally that the only alternative was an amputation. In this condition the sick man visited the Infant, an all-powerful Physician, and begged for a cure.

The merciful Infant heard his prayer. The swelling in the affected member began immediately to disappear, the pain lessened, and in a few days the hand was back to normal condition.

In thanksgiving for his cure, Mr. Achbauer had a gold-plated model of a hand made, an *ex-voto* symbolic of the healing hand of the Infant. Eager to spread devotion, he proposed the chanting of the Litany of the Holy Name of Jesus during the celebration of Mass, a practice you may observe even today. At every opportunity he visited the Infant in His shrine and had Mass offered there.

LXVII

GOOD COMES OF A THEFT COMMITTED AT THE SHRINE

Mysterious but filled with instruction for us are the words Jesus spoke while He was a prisoner in the house of the High Priest. *Ex hoc erit filius hominis sedens a dextris virtutis Dei.* (But henceforth the Son of Man will be seated at the right hand of the power of God— (Luke 22:69). As the Second Person, does Christ not already sit at the right hand of His Father, in solemn council of the Most Holy Trinity? Why, then, does Christ use the term, "From this time on?" For the reason, look into the house of Caiphas, the High Priest. There you will behold a Man who no longer looks human. His face is covered with blood and spittle; He has been mocked and crowned for a fool; His tormentors have branded Him a cheat and a false prophet. Truly could the Father have said, "They disgrace My Son, they rob Him of the honor and glory due Him. And because of this, henceforth He shall sit on my right hand, for His greater honor and glory."

A professional thief committed a daring robbery at the shrine of the Infant. To insure success the robber chose the night time, forcing his way through a high window barricaded with iron, to enter the chapel. He fled with all the precious ornaments of the image, removing even the globe that the Infant holds in His hand. When morning came and the news of the sacrilege spread, worshippers filled the chapel, there to mourn the vandalism. Someone called attention to the cross of solid gold still hanging suspended on the image, a curious thing, since it was easier to remove than the orb and was more precious too, since the globe was copper and gilded, while the cross was pure gold.

After this public disgrace to His Son, God the Father seemingly inspired the faithful to repair the damage by bringing gifts of precious ornaments and money. Requests for Masses multiplied. Attendance at the chapel grew larger than before, and on the Feast of the Holy Name, a sermon was preached at the Masses and Solemn Mass and Vespers sung. "Praise not a man before his death," warns Holy Scripture. The names of many benefactors will be written in the Book of Life, though they go unmentioned here.

The good of the increase of honor and glory coming out of the evil of a robbery did not end here. The fame of the Infant began to extend into foreign lands. Whatever knowledge we have concerning this expansion we shall relate in the following chapters.

LXVIII

THE WORSHIP OF THE INFANT SPREADS TO FOREIGN LANDS

Wherever Joseph, Son of Israel, went, there reigned joy and good fortune. That is why Joseph's father had sent him off to look after his brothers, with the order to "go and see if all be well with your brothers, with the flocks also." (Gen. 37:14) The wise father knew from experience that wherever Joseph went, all would be well. The whole of Egypt came in time to look upon Joseph as their savior, confident of his help in need and danger. To this Holy Scripture testifies: "And the Lord blessed the house of the Egyptian for the sake of Joseph, and made him richer in his home and in the fields." Joseph himself recognized his own worth, saying to his brothers, "God has sent me to deliver you in a striking way." (Gen. 45:7)

Notice the striking similarity between Joseph and our Infant Jesus. Where men worship the Infant, there abide joy and good fortune. We have already pointed out the truth of this in connection with the good people of Prague. Here in Prague the Infant had been disgraced through a robbery. It was God's will now to repair that disgrace, and spread the worship through miracles into other parts of the world.

Requests came in from various countries for some likeness of the Infant. These devout desires were satisfied when replicas made of wax or wood were shipped to Rome, Gratz, Syria, Linz, Upper Austria, and Wiener Neustadt, Austria. Except for Gratz none of these places reported outstanding miracles. Perhaps they were not grateful, nor devout, enough. Yet one can consider this a miracle: that wherever the image of our merciful Infant was sent and honored, there was happiness and the blessings of good fortune. Those who venerated the Infant called Him the "Merciful."

LXIX

A PERSON ACUTELY ILL IS HEALED BY THE INFANT — 1733

Why did our Lord refuse to raise from the dead the daughter of the temple official as long as the crowd of musicians and friends persisted in making a rout, after the manner of Hebrew mourning? Why did He drive these people out of the house with harsh words, as St. Matthew relates? To show, no doubt, that He prefers not the loud and discordant tones of the shawm, but the sound of loving hearts raised in simple prayer. Where He finds these, He is disposed even to raise the dead, as He demonstrated.

This recalls an event of 1733. The Convent of the Order of Poor Clares in Gratz, Styria, had received a replica of the Infant that had been touched to the original image in Prague. They reported a number of benefactions, one of them concerned with the critically ill twenty-two-year-old daughter of the Handl family. This young girl had been given the last rites when the image was brought upon request to her bedside. Soothed into a deep sleep, she wakened refreshed and able to leave her sickbed. With simple faith and joy she called out, "Let me get up, the Infant Jesus has restored my health." At first her relatives considered her hysterical. But the doctor's examination found the girl completely better, and he himself called the cure miraculous. Blessed be the Infant for this, and similar other favors recorded of an image touched to the original one in Prague.

LXX

A WATER SHORTAGE IS RELIEVED, THANKS TO THE INFANT — 1736

We know from natural experience that flint when struck, will give off sparks. Not so the rock in Horeb which Moses struck with his rod. *Egresse sunt aquae largissimae.* Moses struck this rock in the wilderness twice, and twice it gave forth water.

This rock, this flint, is a symbol of our merciful Infant Jesus. St. Paul testified, *"Petra autem erat Christus."* (The rock was Christ.) But if the divine

Ballerini's conception of Venerable Father Cyril of the Mother of God, the first promoter of the devotion to the Infant of Prague.

Maria Manriquez de Lara, wife of Count Vratislav Pernstyn, who brought the statue of the Infant of Prague as an heirloom from Spain in 1556. Seated, is her daughter, Polyxena. This painting by Sanchez Coello is in Roudnice Castle, Czechoslovakia.

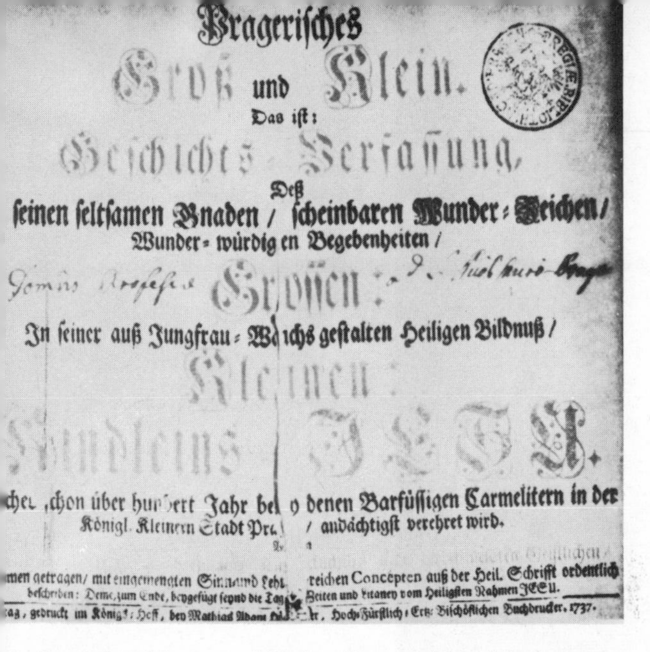

Pragerisches
Groß und Klein.
Das ist:
Geschichts-Verfassung,
Deß
seinen seltsamen Gnaden / scheinbaren Wunder-Zeichen /
Wunder-würdig en Begebenheiten /
Grossen:
In seiner auß Jungfrau-Wachs gestalten Heiligen Bildnuß /
Kleinen:
Kindleins JESU.
...chon über hundert Jahr bey denen Barfüssigen Carmelitern in der
Königl. Kleinern Stadt Pr... / andächtigst verehret wird.
...men getragen / mit eingemengten Sinn- und Lehr-reichen Concepten auß der Heil. Schrifft ordentlich
beschrieben: Deme, zum Ende, beygefügt seynd die Tag-Zeiten und Litaney vom Heiligsten Nahmen JESU.
...ag, gedruckt im Königl. Hoff, bey Mathias Adam ...r, Hoch-Fürstlich-Ertz-Bischöflichen Buchdrucker, 1737.

simile of the title page of Father Emmerich's original manu-
pt, *Pragerisches Gross und Klein* of 1737.

Representation of the Infant of Prague as it appears in the original manuscript of 1737, preserved in Charles University library in Prague.

These are four of twenty-tw paintings from the eighteenth cen tury preserved in the rectory o Our Lady of Victory in Prague.

Princess Polyxena Lobkowitz depicted presenting the statue of the Infant of Prague to the Discalced Carmelites in 1628.

The Blessed Mother as she appeared in 1638 to Venerable Father Cyril and presented him with funds for the repair of the statue.

Discalced Carmelites seek refuge in the Infant of Prague at the time of the plague of 1713.

Countess Benigna Catherine Lobkowitz offering Father Cyril the means to finance the building of Our Lady of Victory Church in 1642.

The miraculous Image in its shrine in Prague.

Two crowns preserved in Our Lady of Victory Church. These are the work of Prague artists.

Wax statue of the Infant of Pilsen, as it appears in the Infant of Prague Shrine in Pilsen. This copy of the Prague original was made about the end of the seventeenth century.

Santo Bambino of Saint Vincent Pallotti in the Church of S. Salvatore in Onda.

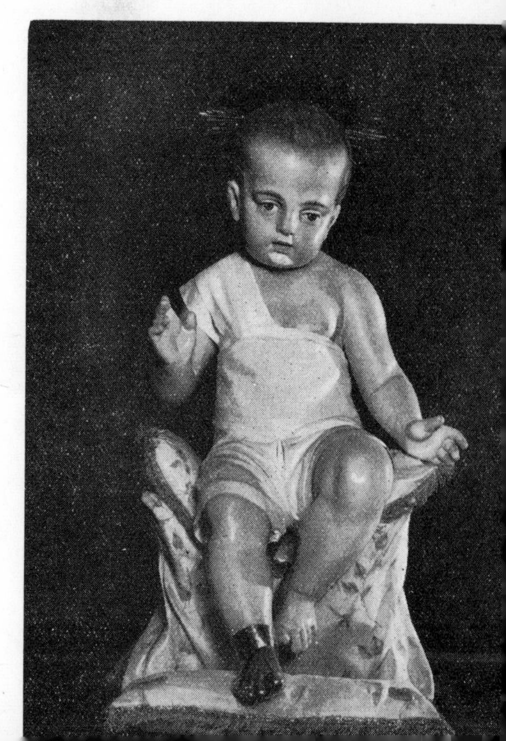

Santo Nino de Cebu, Philippines. The oldest known representation of the Christ Child as a King, it has been venerated in the Church of the Augustinian Fathers in Cebu since 1521.

Santo Bambino of Salerno (1600).

Roi de Gloire (The King of Glory) venerated in the Carmel of Beaune by Venerable Sister Margaret of the Blessed Sacrament.

Enfant Jésus of Prague, in the sanctuary of the Barnabite Fathers, Brussels, Belgium.

The Holy Child of Earth and Heaven
in St. Patrick's Cathedral, New York.

Miniature statue of the Infant of Prague as it appears in the Lilliputian Palace of The Doll House of Colleen Moore. This is now housed in the Museum of Science and Industry, Chicago, Illinois.

Charles Cardinal Kasper, Archbishop of Prague, as he blesses a statute of the Infant of Prague, January 2, 1937, for the people of Argentina. To the Cardinal's right is the Franciscan missionary, Father Joachim Buchazha, who took the statue to Argentina. To the Cardinal's left is Monsignor Vladyka.

The miraculous statue of the Infant of Prague dressed in the vestments donated by Empress Maria Theresa.

Outdoor monument to the Infant of Prague at the National Shrine of the Infant of Prague, St. Wenceslaus Church, Prague, Oklahoma.

The statue of the Infant in the Chapel of Sts. Cyril and Methodius in Jerusalem. It is offset against a plaque background depicting the cathedrals of each Archbishop and Bishop in Czechoslovakia. Both chapel and statue were built with funds donated by the Czech hierarchy.

A new interpretation of the Infant of Prague carved by Dr. Suzanne Silvercruys. Carved of linden wood and standing about two and a half feet tall, it is in the Church of St. Philip in Warrenville, Conn.

rock is struck by the steel of ingratitude and sin, it will throw off sparks of just anger. Struck with the rod of sincere confidence and true devotion, it will provide waters of abundant grace.

An example of the latter is drawn from a letter received from the previously mentioned convent in Gratz, Styria, which we here quote: "Our Infant Jesus continues to be merciful to us, His miserable servants. We have placed Him upon the high altar in the choir close to the Blessed Sacrament. Holy Mass has been celebrated in His honor and many prayers offered to bring about the end of a water shortage in our convent since last fall. We now have water in abundance."

LXXI
THE INFANT HEALS A SEVERE CASE OF FEBRIS MILIARIS—1736

"Who touched Me?" Christ asked the question as He stood in the midst of a crowd. Such a touch could have been accidental. If this had been the case, our Lord would not have asked the question. No, the touch was deliberate, an act of faith on the part of the woman suffering from hemorrhage. "I know that I radiate power," Christ Himself has said. Like the woman healed of her infirmity, we too can touch Jesus and experience His wondrous mercy.

A further miracle reported from the Gratz convent concerns a little boy dying of *febris miliaris.*

There was no hope at all for his recovery. But once again the replica touched to the miraculous image of Prague was brought from the convent and laid upon the sick child. His fever left instantly and he suffered no ill effects.

LXXII

A STUBBORN SINNER IS CONVERTED THROUGH THE INFANT — 1736

The gospel narratives give three acounts of Jesus raising the dead to life. The daughter of Jairus he commanded with few words: "Girl, I say to thee, arise!" To the son of the widow of Naim on his way to burial, He addressed similar words, "Young man, I say to thee, arise." But Lazarus he raised after he had been buried four days, groaning within Himself, crying out with a loud voice, and tears: *"Infremuit, lacrimatus, clamavit."* How can we explain these differences?

The young girl lying dead in her own home symbolizes sin committed by thought; the dead youth carried out of his house, sin committed in deed. But the already buried Lazarus symbolizes habitual sin, which renders the sinner incapable of remorse and repentance. In the examples we have cited, Jesus teaches a method of dealing with sinners. To those who have offended in thought, one or two words suffice. But the man habituated to sinful deeds needs to be touched, and all the more so, the more stubborn has the sinner become through the years.

A man hardened in sin came to confession to one of our Fathers, who used both severity and kindness to turn him from his evil ways. But the effort was in vain. The penitent was moved neither by appeals to the mercy of God nor threats of His justice. He would make no promise of amendment. "Father I am done for. I know it. I haven't the strength or the will power to fight this thing." The confessor exacted just one favor: the man was to go into the chapel of the Infant and pray in this fashion: "O merciful Infant Jesus, have pity on me! Show me the way; let me do what my Confessor wants me to do!"

Such was the merciful love of the Infant that the penitent returned deeply touched to the confessional, where he made a good confession. Thus were fulfilled the words of the prophet Ezechiel, "When the wicked man turns away from the wickedness that he has committed, he shall not die. And I will not mention his wickedness to him."

LXXIII

THE INFANT AS MIRACULOUS PHYSICIAN ATTENDS THE SICKBED OF A CHILD 1736-1737

Experience has often proved the truth of the adage: "Birds of a feather flock together." The wicked tend to seek the company of other wicked, to their mutual misfortune, but the innocent love the company of the innocent. It is not surprising, then, to learn that little children were always welcomed by the Savior: "Let them come unto Me." If they were in need of healing, the Master put forth His hand, and they were healed, says St. Luke.

In 1736 the young son of Mrs. Maria Anna Buckein became very ill. His high fever and complications had produced convulsions, resulting in crossed eyes and twisted limbs. When the patient was a baby, his mother had recommended him to the Infant Jesus, Who helped him during teething periods and a case of measles. Filled with trust, the mother brought this more serious case to the Infant, promising special prayers in thanksgiving, and the offering for a Holy Mass. This Mass was celebrated in the chapel of the Infant. At this same time the sick child began to improve, and later fully recovered. This was a great mercy, indeed, but not the only one.

In the following year the same mother returned home to find her young son, John Joseph, weeping with pain after a fall. Examination discovered a hernia, which was temporarily eased by bandaging. But again the pious mother took her problem to the Infant, and once more the Infant stretched forth His hand in healing. The next morning there was no need for the bandage, although only a single night had intervened, too short a time for nature to have healed the disorder. The mother attributed her son's miraculous cure to the divine Physician, our Infant Jesus.

LXXIV

THE INFANT CURES A WOMAN AFFLICTED WITH TUBERCULOSIS

St. John narrates the visit of Jesus, the divine Physician, to the pool Bethsaida, where He found among the lame and the blind and the consumptive, a man afflicted with palsy. This man complained, not so much about his physical sufferings, as his distress at having been abandoned by his friends. "*Hominem non habeo.*" "I have no one when the waters are moved to lower me down into the pool." (John 5:7) I found no reason for wonder that, among the hundreds of spectators here, only one, the sympathetic Jesus, spoke out. "Rise," He commanded the sick man, "take up thy pallet and walk." This is the way of our loving Savior. Where human help fails, He is ready with divine assistance.

Kindness such as this, a woman suffering a withered limb experienced in our own day. Like the man of the gospel she could also say, "I have no one, Lord, to help me." But she made her way to the chapel of the Infant, a pond of mercy, and was fortified to make her confession and receive Holy Communion. This spiritual miracle was followed by another. The woman felt the afflicted leg return to normal. She took an oath testifying to this miracle, though there is no record of the case in the official records. The reason for this we cannot explain, nor even divulge the name of the penitent who experienced this mercy.

LXXV

THE INFANT JESUS SUITS HIS COUNTENANCE TO THE OCCASION

There is a scene in the Apocalypse where one of the twenty-four elders comforts John: "Do not weep, behold the lion of the tribe of Juda has overcome to open the scroll and its seven seals." (Apoc. 5:5) At this the visionary lifts his eyes, expecting to see the lion, but beholds instead, a lamb standing in the midst of the elders. Can this Lamb be also the Lion? Yes, both are Christ seated on the throne of judgment. At one time, He is the Lion, punishing sinful man; at another He is the Lamb, showing him mercy.

So does the Infant act upon occasion. With those who disgrace His name He deals as a lion. To those who honor and praise Him, He shows the meekness of a lamb. It is not an easy thing to prove such a change of countenance, yet I think I can attempt it. No likeness of the Infant reproduces Him exactly. I, the writer, have purposely questioned persons concerning their impression of the face of the Infant. A particular occasion in mind, some reported that He looked "grim and angry." The same persons recalled that on another day He appeared filled with loving kindness. I repeated my inquiry to different groups, none of whom has occasion to talk it over with others previous to my questioning.

To cite a case in point: a woman visited the chapel, curious at what she had heard of the miraculous image. As she gazed upon it, the face of the Infant was obscured by a thick haze; she could scarcely see the garments covering the figure. Wondering and frightened, she concluded that it was her many unforgiven sins that obstructed her vision. She made a sincere confession and returned. Even yet, there was but partial vision. Consulting her confessor again, she was advised to make a general confession. This she did, and returning to the image she was able to see the face of the image. But only for a short time, when the darkness of a mist overshadowed it again. She begged the Infant for light to recall a hidden sin still unconfessed. Oh, the infinite mercy of God! Once again she returned from the confessional, able to gaze on the Infant and enjoy there His sweet and friendly smile, not the lion of justice, but the lamb of mercy. This story the woman confided to her father confessor, declaring it under oath to be true. May the merciful Infant Jesus be forever blessed!

This historical account comes to an end with what we have reported thus far. We ask all lovers and devotees of the merciful Infant Jesus to report whatever special graces they may have received, or will receive in the future, through veneration of the holy image, to the Discalced Carmelites of our monastery, St. Mary of Victory in Less Side, Prague. By expressing their gratitude these persons will increase the honor due to the holy image, at the same time meriting additional graces for themselves.

CHAPTER 5

HISTORICAL PRAYERS TO THE GREAT AND LITTLE ONE OF PRAGUE

Since the historical prayers to the Great and Little One had been in use in the Church of Our Lady of Victory from the beginning of the devotion, and cannot be ascribed to Father Emmerich, nevertheless, they are an integral part of his manuscript, *Pragerisches Gross und Klein*. The unique spirit of this devotion is beautifully expressed in the lines of the following prayers:

Little Office of the Most Holy Name of Jesus

MATINS

V. May the Name of the Lord be praised
R. Now and forever. Amen.
V. Lord, open Thou my lips
R. And my mouth shall declare Thy praise.
V. O God, come to my assistance
R. O Lord, make haste to help me.
V. Glory be to the Father, and to the Son, and to the Holy Ghost
R. As it was in the beginning, is now and ever shall be, world without end. Amen.

HYMN

O sweetest Jesus, when I think of Thee
Self is lost—Thy love is joy untold,
No mortal thing such sweetness brings to me
As Thy dear presence, Lord, all wealth enfolds.

Ant. He humbled Himself and became obedient unto death — yes, even to the death of the cross. Therefore, has God exalted Him and given Him a Name which is above all names, that in the name of Jesus, every knee should bend, in heaven, on earth, and under the earth.

V. The whole earth should adore and praise Thee.
R. They shall praise Thy name.

Let us pray: O God, Who hast ordained Thy only begotten Son as Saviour of the human race, and called His Name, Jesus, grant we beseech Thee, that we, who honor Thy name here on earth, may enjoy the beatific vision in heaven, through the same Jesus Christ, Thy Son, our Lord, Who liveth and reigneth with Thee in the unity of the Holy Spirit, forever and ever. Amen.

PRIME

V. May the Name of the Lord be praised.
R. Now and forever. Amen.
V. O God, come to my assistance
R. O Lord, make haste to help me.
V. Glory be, etc.

HYMN

No sweeter song can humans sing
Than song of Thee, O Jesus!
Nothing more joyous can human ears
Perceive than Thou, O Jesus.
No sweeter thought can man conceive
Than only Thou, my Jesus!
No better wish can fill man's heart
Than Thou alone, O Jesus!

Ant. (As in Matins)

TIERCE

V. The Name of the Lord be praised
R. Now and forever. Amen.
V. O God, come to my assistance
R. O Lord, make haste to help me.

HYMN

O gentle Jesus, hope of sinful soul,
From morn till night our solace is in Thee,
Who seeks Thee, Lord, finds help at every hour.
What rapture will be his, when last he rests in Thee.

Ant. (As in Matins)

SEXT

V. (As in Tierce)

HYMN

With Thee alone, O Jesus, lies true joy of heart,
With Thee alone, O Jesus, all fear and pain depart,

From Thee alone, O living Fount, all sweetness flows,
From Thee, O lovely Sun, each beam of grace doth flow.
Ant. (As in Matins)

NONE

V. (As in Tierce)

HYMN

No tongue of mortal can express,
No pen can write the blessedness,
Whoever once hath proved it, knows,
What bliss from love of Jesus flows.
Ant. (As in Matins)

VESPERS

V. (As in Tierce)

HYMN

No earthly kingdom like to Thine, O Jesus, my King,
Thy burden lighter, Thy yoke sweeter, than earthly thing
O were I only in Thy kingdom above,
Forever Thee to praise and Thee to love.
Ant. (As in Matins)

COMPLINE

V. May the Name of the Lord be praised
R. Now and forever. Amen.
V. Convert us, O God, our Saviour

R. And turn away Thine anger from us.
V. O God come to my assistance.
R. O Lord, make haste to help us.
V. Glory be, etc.

HYMN

Stay with us, Jesus, Lord, we pray,
In life's dark night, be Thou our stay,
Dispel earth's gloom, with Thy joy fill
The world, in bondage to Thy sweet will.
Ant. (As in Matins)

CLOSING HYMN

Now, my task fulfilled, the prayerful hours complete,
O Jesus, for Thy great goodness, my thanks replete,
From wiles of evil foe, I beg Thee deign,
To keep me safe, till Thee in Heaven I gain.

LITANY OF THE MOST SWEET NAME OF JESUS

300 days indulgence — Pope Sixtus V
July 11, 1587

Lord, have mercy on us
Christ have mercy on us
Lord, have mercy on us
Christ, hear us
Christ, graciously hear us
God, the Father of heaven Have mercy on us!
God, the Son, Redeemer of the World

God the Holy Ghost — Have mercy on us!
Holy Trinity, one God
Jesus, Son of the living God
Jesus, Son of the Virgin Mary
Jesus, mighty God
Jesus, most powerful
Jesus, most perfect
Jesus, most worthy of praise
Jesus, most wonderful
Jesus, most lovable
Jesus, most loving
Jesus, brighter than the stars
Jesus, more beautiful than the Moon
Jesus, brighter than the Sun
Jesus, most humble
Jesus, most mild
Jesus, most patient
Jesus, most obedient
Jesus, most sweet
Jesus, lover of chastity
Jesus, our joy and our love
Jesus, King of peace
Jesus, Mirror of the interior life
Jesus, Example of all virtues
Jesus, zealous for souls
Jesus, our Refuge
Jesus, Father of the poor
Jesus, Comforter of the afflicted
Jesus, Treasure of the faithful
Jesus, a precious Gem
Jesus, a Treasury of perfection

Jesus, good Shepherd Have mercy on us!
Jesus, Star of the sea
Jesus, true Light of the world
Jesus, Eternal Wisdom
Jesus, Infinite Goodness
Jesus, Joy of the angels
Jesus, King of patriarchs
Jesus, Ruler of prophets
Jesus, Master of apostles
Jesus, Teacher of evangelists
Jesus, Strength of martyrs
Jesus, Light of confessors
Jesus, Spouse of virgins
Jesus, Crown of all saints
Be merciful Spare us, O Jesus
Be merciful Deliver us, O Jesus
From all evil Deliver us, O Jesus
From all sin
From Thy wrath
From the snares of the devil
From the transgression of Thy commandments
From the attack of all enemies
Through Thy holy Incarnation
Through Thy holy Coming
Through Thy holy Birth
Through Thy holy Circumcision
Through Thy pain and labor
Through Thy scourging
Through Thy holy death
Through Thy holy Resurrection
Through Thy holy Ascension
Through Thy holy Coronation

Through Thy glory Deliver us, O Jesus
Through the intercession of Thy holy Mother and Virgin
Through the intercession of all the Saints
Lamb of God, Who takest, etc. (3 times)
Jesus, Hear us
Jesus, graciously hear us
Our Father
Lord, hear my prayer
And let my cry come unto Thee.

Let us pray: O almighty and eternal God, Who through the glorious Name of Thy dear Son, our Lord Jesus Christ, hast filled the hearts of the faithful with the greatest consolation and sweetness and hast made the evil spirits fear and tremble, grant, we beseech Thee, that all who devoutly honor the holy Name of Jesus, Thy Son, our Lord, Who livest and reignest, one God, world without end. Amen.

V. The name of the Lord be praised
R. Both now and forever.

PRAYER TO THE MOST LOVING INFANT JESUS

O most loving and blessed Infant Jesus!—Thou great God and Lord of heaven and earth, Who hast clothed and hidden Thy Divine Majesty under the lovable semblance of a child before Whom the powers of the heavens tremble, the mighty kings of the earth bow and the evil spirits under the earth must bend; Who through the Almighty God, for love of us hast become a little Child, so that we might love Thee more ardently and serve Thee more faithfully and humbly follow Thy example in childlike purity and love.

I, a poor sinner, bow down humbly before the great God concealed in this lovable Child and adore Thee! I love Thee as the highest and most loving God; I entrust myself to Thy infinite Goodness. O teach me after Thy example to love humility and crush pride, to desire to grow in virtue and childlike trust; direct and rule me and make me virtuous, that I may please Thee and be little in this world and great in the next. Amen.

NINE PIOUS PRAYERS IN HONOR OF THE FIVE SENSES AND MEMBERS OF THE BODY OF THE MOST HOLY INFANT JESUS

FIRST PRAYER

In Honor of the Sacred Head

Be praised a thousand times, O all-holy Head of my dearest Infant Jesus! More costly than all gold, nobler and more shining than all the gems of the whole earth, at whose least beck or nod, heaven and earth, yes, even hell must bow in humble obedience, before Whom all the great rulers of this world must tremble, fear, and humble themselves,

O mighty, little Jesus! Therefore, I, a poor sinner, with contrite heart adore Thy Divine Head, which is the Treasure-house of all wisdom and knowledge, wishing with all my heart that all people in the whole world might acknowledge Thee, O my loving little Jesus, as their highest and only Ruler, that they might love Thee, fear and honor Thee and unceasingly praise and adore Thee with eternal thanksgiving. O dearest Jesus, Thou little Child, my Lord and my God, never permit me to forsake Thee, but dying to my own will, I may always follow Thy adorable will in all things and never deviate from it in the smallest detail. Amen.

Glory be to the Father, etc.

O most lovable Infant Jesus
May I never from Thee depart
Take my heart and give me Thine
Let both hearts be but one heart.

SECOND PRAYER

In honor of the Most Lovable,
Shining Eyes of Jesus.

Be praised with a loving kiss, O starlike, shining Eyes of the most lovable Infant Jesus, my Saviour. O, that I might worship Thee with a hundred thousand kisses and the adorations that are due Thee! You, Who drive away all darkness of sin from the hearts of men, enlighten every man who comes into this world, behold, O most loving Infant God, me, a poor sinner and have pity on me! Enlighten me, Thy unworthy servant, that I may fulfill all justice. O sweetest Jesus, deign to look with Thy loving eyes upon all who are in the darkness and shadow of death, that they may attain to the knowledge of Thy eternal truth. Grant that I may always guard my eyes and turn them away from the vanities of this world and unceasingly raise them to Thee, Who art in heaven. Amen.

Glory be to the Father, etc. (as above)

THIRD PRAYER
To the Most Tender Ears of Jesus

Be praised forevermore, and be adored, O most lovable and most tender Ears of my dearest Infant Jesus! O most loving Child! Listen attentively to my pleading voice, hear my supplication in all my anxieties, troubles and misfortunes. O most loving Jesus, do not close Thy benign ears to my pleadings and those of all poor sinners in their temporal and spiritual necessities, but deign to hear us. O most tender Infant Jesus, incline Thy most compassionate ears to me, Thy unworthy servant, who daily waits and watches at Thy door, that he may be graciously heard often and until he arrives at eternal life and attains, O most loving Redeemer, eternal salvation. Amen.

Glory be to the Father, etc. (as above)

FOURTH PRAYER
To the Rose-Red Lips of Jesus

Be praised among all the sons of men, O most beautiful, adorable Infant Jesus, upon whose Rose-

Red Lips, grace has overflowed. I devoutly kiss your most sweet cheeks. O speak to me, my Lord and my God, and I, Thy unworthy servant, shall gladly obey Thee. May Thy sweet voice sound in my ears. O Divine Child, Thy voice is sweeter than honey and we are drawn after Thee in the odor of Thy ointments to love Thee ardently. O all-loving Infant Saviour, teach me to observe Thy most Holy Will and place before my mouth a guard and about the portals of my lips a shield. Do not permit that one unbecoming word escape me that may displease either Thee or my neighbor; grant that my speech may always be such as to show my ardent love for Thee and that it may always edify my neighbor. Amen.

Glory be to the Father, etc. (as above)

FIFTH PRAYER

To the Most Loving Breast and Love-Inflamed Heart of Jesus

Be praised a thousand times with an ardent kiss, O Loving Breast and love-inflamed little Heart of my sweetest Infant Jesus. I pray Thee, through this adorable Heart to create in me a new heart and renew in it an ardent spirit, so that I may will nothing, seek nothing, and love nothing, outside of Thee. O most loving Child, permit me to rest on Thy love-inflamed Heart with Thy most beloved disciple, John. Let me always rest on Thy Heart, let me live in Thee and die in Thee and remain united to Thee for all eternity. O sweetest Jesus, take my heart, which I offer and give to Thee. In exchange give me Thine, so that I no longer live, but that You may live in me, through Thy most divine Heart. Amen.

Glory be to the Father, etc. (as above)

SIXTH PRAYER

To the Right Hand of Jesus

Be praised forevermore with a loving kiss, O tender Right Hand of my most beautiful Jesus, the instrument of all gifts and graces! O most amiable Child, stretch forth and open Thy Hand to me in all my necessities and miseries, so that enriched by Thy bounty, I may not appear before Thee empty-handed. May Thy right hand guide me on the path of all justice, ardent devotion and true virtue. Have mercy on me, O most adorable Jesus, because I am needy and poor; place me on the day of judgment on Thy right hand, separated from the damned and placed among the sheep of the blessed, I may hope to be called to the heavenly mansions and to eternal beatitude. Amen.

Glory be, etc. (As above)

SEVENTH PRAYER

To the Left Hand of Jesus

Be praised a thousand times, O little Left Hand of my dearest Infant Jesus! I humbly beg Thee to place Thy left hand under my head, so that it may softly rest thereon and do Thou receive me in my anxieties, pain, and sickness and in my last agony. Come to my assistance, so that I may suffer all misfortunes patiently, joyfully, and gratefully out of love for Thee and may they all redound to Thy greater glory, O most patient Infant Saviour. Amen.

Glory be, etc. (As above)

EIGHTH PRAYER

In Honor of the Weak Little Shoulders of Jesus

Be praised a thousand times, O weak little Shoulders of the all-powerful Infant Saviour. I implore Thee from the bottom of my heart, O almighty Child, that Thou wouldst take me, Thy erring sheep, upon Thy invincible Shoulders and carry me into the heavenly fold to enjoy forever the watchful care of the Eternal Good Shepherd. Amen.

Glory be, etc. (As above)

NINTH PRAYER

In Honor of the Grace-Laden Feet of Jesus

Be praised a thousand times on bended knee and prostrate upon the ground, O well-beloved blessed Feet of the Infant Saviour. Would that I had never strayed from the right path, but had remained faithful to Thee. Direct and guide my steps on the way that leads to Thee, Who art the Way, the Truth, and the Life. May I never wander from the straight and narrow path that leads to Thee, and may I follow the light of eternal life leading to the realms of bliss above. Amen.

Glory be, etc. (As above)

OFFERING

O most loving Infant Jesus! The prayers we have just said we offer to Thy adorable Heart. Do Thou perfect them and make them worthy of Thy Divine Majesty. We also offer Thee all the words, affections and intentions with which Thy Holy Mother and St. Joseph worshipped Thee in Thy childhood. We join our prayers with the adoration of the holy angels, the simple shepherds, the three Holy Kings from the East; yes, with that of all the faithful Christians in the whole world. In thanksgiving for all the graces and benefits we have received, we humbly beg Thee that Thou wouldst forgive us our sins through the merits of Thy holy birth and life, and lead us to the haven of eternal blessedness. Amen.

PART III

CHAPTER 6

THE GREAT AND LITTLE ONE OF PRAGUE IN MODERN HISTORY

After due consideration concerning the Great and Little One of Prague in its early history by men eminently capable of recording it with exactitude —Venerable Father Cyril of the Mother of God, and Father Emmerich of St. Stephen—it remains for us to uncover the pages of the Holy Child of Prague in modern history in order to understand completely the revelation of the Little One of Prague as the Great One in the history of mankind.

Father Emmerich's account covers approximately[1] the entire period in which the Discalced Carmelites of Prague exercised their guardianship of the shrine of the Infant of Prague until 1784 when, victimized by the reformistic vandalism of Emperor Joseph II, they were forced to leave. It is little wonder that this devotion to the Holy Child of Prague was among the first to suffer from the vandalism of the periods of the Enlightenment and Josephinism. It is evident that this devotion, a sublime product of Carmelite mysticism, would have to assume a position in direct conflict with the rationalistic trends prevailing toward the end of the eighteenth century and the beginning of the nineteenth century. Through the message of *Pragerisches Gross und Klein* this devotion was kept from oblivion, for when the time of trial arrived, the devotion had already been established. A decline was indeed noticeable, but fortunately the devotion was sufficiently strong to survive the crises of the times and to come to the fullness of its glory as it is known in the twentieth century.

Another reason for this development is the exceptional attraction of the Infant of Prague as it faithfully symbolizes the Holy Child—the King, so evident in its impressive representation. The spiritual concept of the Kingship of the Holy Child could hardly be more artistically portrayed. History shows that there were various representations[2] which preceded the Holy Child of Prague, but none caught and held the universal appeal as did this image. Even those following it were never able to achieve its popularity, and so one may conclude that the historical appearance of the Infant of Prague, as we know it, is unique in its appeal.

It is necessary to view the decline of this devotion under pressure of Josephinism as a part of the general decline of all religious belief which the rationalistic mind of the time was too proud to accept. One can visualize the concern of the Discalced Carmelites in Prague at the cool treatment accorded their spiritual treasure. Truly, if at any period human reason needed the lesson of littleness and humility it was this one which had replaced the theocentric attitude of previous centuries with the egocentricity of rationalism.

It is not our purpose to detail all of the spirit of the time, with its political, cultural, and religious implications. Rather, it is sufficient to note its reflections in the general decadence of the devotion and zeal of the time. The disparity between religious theory and practice was so great that religious indifferentism became one of the marks of the time, to the detriment of devotion.

During this time convents and monasteries had been secularized and confiscated for public purposes such as, schools, hospitals, and office buildings. It is interesting to note that the Church of Our Lady of Victory with its shrine of the Infant of Prague was reserved for ecclesiastical[3] use and given the status of a parish church on September 25, 1784. Even state officials were forced, albeit unwillingly, to reconcile themselves to the acceptance of the popularity of the devotion. It was at this time that the guardianship of the shrine was transferred to the priests of the Order of St. John of Jerusalem, better known as the Knights of Malta, who were considered by government officials to be more modern, flexible and suitable to the sentiments of the times than were the Carmelite Mendicants. Fortunately for the devotion, the first pastor, Father John Raymund, appointed December 5, 1784, patterned his administration on the Carmelite tradition.

Born and raised in Prague, Father Raymund was well aware of the tradition and mission contained within the devotion to the Infant.[4] He was renowned as an orator and his sermons were constantly directed toward a spiritual revival. The historical account, *Kurtzer Bericht von dem Ursprung und Bewardnus der Kirche Mariae de Victoria, welche ehemals ab Ao 1624-1787 die unbeschuhten Karmeliten in der kleineren Stadt Prag innen gehavt und bedienent,*[5] further attests to the fidelity of Father John Raymund to the Carmelite ideal of promoting devotion to the Infant of Prague. While he observed all the traditions connected with devotion to the Infant, there is no evidence that he contributed anything to the material decoration of either the church or shrine. It was this latter element that no doubt accounts for the scant attention given him by some contemporary historians, although his spiritual and literary endeavors were contributions of a high order. His historical research left an invaluable record relating to the miraculous intervention of the Infant of Prague during the reign of Joseph II. While the immediate transfer of guardianship of the shrine was unmarked by any drastic change, the situation was not long to endure. Following the death of Father John Raymund in 1808, devotion to the Infant Jesus waned, and through poverty and neglect the church of Our Lady of Victory fell into disrepair. Sharing the fate of other magnificent churches built in the Baroque era, the church of Our Lady of Victory lost its functional purpose of accommodating worshippers and became instead an artistic monument and tourist attraction.

With Catholicism hampered by the existing ideology of state theocracy which formed the background of the reforms of Joseph II, the result was a noticeable decline in the devotion and zeal of the faithful. Even at the shrine of the Infant of Prague this spiritual apathy was evident, despite the efforts of Father John Raymund.

Hope for improved conditions was revived when Leopold II, the brother of Joseph II, ascended the throne. It was during the brief two-year reign that the innovations imposed by his brother on the Austrian empire were recanted. During the subsequent reigns of Francis (1792-1835) and Ferdinand V (1835-1848) the Church in Bohemia was revitalized. The years of oppression had taken their toll, however, and simple devotions like that of the Infant Jesus of Prague had lost their popularity so that the veneration, while not dying out completely, was considerably diminished in Prague. Despite the unsettled conditions of the times, the devotion spread to many other countries of Europe. At this time, Europe could hardly be considered a choice atmosphere for the development of the devotion, since the forces of irreligion in France, Italy and the low countries proved a hindrance to the influence that the Carmelites might otherwise have exercised in spreading devotion to the Holy Child-the King. In France, the defamation of churches and the degrading manner in which the victory of reason over "superstition" was celebrated indicates the direction of the revolution in that country. The plight of Pope Pius VI, imprisoned and transported in a dying condition to Valence, and the tragic history of Pope Pius VII under the regime of

Napoleon, who continued the disruption of religious orders and congregations, is indicative of the involvment of Italy in the disorder of the times.[6]

The foregoing consideration of the various forces fomenting in Europe should suffice as an explanation for the temporary eclipse of the devotion to the Infant Jesus of Prague by the spirit of the times, and the reason its re-establishment by the fathers of the Knights of Malta proved such a formidable task.

On the occasion of the renovation of the Church of Our Lady of Victory (1882), the zealous new pastor, Father John Slansky, took advantage of the opportunity to make improvements in the shrine of the Infant of Prague. For this work he called the best artists of the time. Pietro Ciani built a new altar later gilted by Joseph Nejtek. When the work was completed,[7] the miraculous statue was transferred to its new abode with elaborate ecclesiastical ceremonial. And yet with all the material embellishments the public had not been brought to their Divine King, for a chronicle records the fact that the shrine remained empty of worshippers most of the time, although devotions were carried on "in the solemn manner" of the liturgy.

Thus it was that for the first time the Infant of Prague was called on to show Himself as the Good Financier.[8] Funds were insufficient to cover the cost of the extensive renovations, and Father Slansky, dressing the Infant as a beggar equipped with the traditional bag for alms, sent the Image on a tour of the various monasteries in Prague. The Infant's brief stay in the various shrines served two purposes: alms sufficient to cover the cost of the renovations were generously donated, and the popularity the devotion had previously enjoyed was once again rekindled, with attention being directed to the fact that the Infant was to be honored as the King.

Noting the extraordinary intervention of the Holy Child of Prague, Father Slansky organized an apostolate to spread the devotion. In 1879 twelve religious orders and congregations joined in a united effort to promote the honor of the Little King. This included solemn processions, and sermons by the best orators of the day. This public profession of faith in the Infant was marked by a spiritual revival. In 1882, Father Slansky arranged for murals depicting the history of the Holy Child of Prague and the first Carmelite promotors of the devotion, and through the interest thus awakened in the field of liturgical art succeeded in furthering the apostolate. The principal events thus portrayed[9] were those described in *Pragerisches Gross und Klein*. All the work is believed to have been done by Schmidt, only a part of which remains intact at the present time. The Czech artist, Louis Simek, was commissioned in the same year to design and sculpture replicas of the Infant in order to supply the great demand on both domestic and foreign markets. Immigrants to all parts of the world, and principally to the United States, through their continuing demand for replicas and other devotionals, were instrumental in spreading the devotion to all parts of the earth.

Perhaps the greatest impetus given to the re-establishment of the glory of the Great and Little One of Prague was the steadily increasing amount of literature written on the subject. This took form in books, pamphlets, leaflets and prayerbooks, which together with many historical contributions, served to disseminate the knowledge of the Child-the King. To detail the scope of this literature would prove a monumental task. It is sufficient for our purpose to consider only those contributions that exerted a decisive influence on the devotion.

Father Joseph Mayer, a Redemptorist, led the literature of the revival with a history of the devotion compiled in 1883. Entitled *Das gnadenreiche Jesukind in der Kirche Sancta Maria de Victoria zu Prag,* this edition had a circulation of twenty-five thousand copies. The following year a Czech edition was published in Prague. This publication proved to be so popular that Americans of Czech descent in St. Louis reprinted it in the newspaper *Hlas* (Voice) in 1885. Despite the fact that Father Mayer borrowed extensively from Emmerich's *Pragerisches Gross und Klein,* the stimulus given by this timely book was impressive. There is much to admire in its vivid style, shrewd combination of historical and hagiological events, and solid evaluation of the nineteenth century. Among its many records it includes sworn statements concerning favors received from the Infant, attesting to the miraculous character of the Image. For more than a century and a half, Emmerich's historical outlook was enriched[10] by Mayer's critical analysis of events between 1735 and 1884, and the work of this author was to awaken and influence literary interest in the subject in other lands. Many periodicals carried his stories either in their entirety or in condensed form.

In 1889, the Belgian Carmelites of Namur published an abridged French translation which was later elaborated and re-edited in 1893 and 1894. This *Histoire de la statue miraculeuse du Saint Enfant Jésus de Prague,* written by a Discalced Carmelite nun, is a valuable contribution, although it was dependent on Emmerich's account as the source of information. The great literary contribution of Gabrielle Fontaine merits special mention. Her *Histoire de l'Enfant Jesus Miraculeux de Prague,* published for the first time in 1895, reached its fifth revision in 1908. Her information was collected in Prague from Emmerich's account. Nevertheless she produced an independent historical account. Her devotion found expression in a practical way through the *Manuel de Prières,* which contained the daily prayers, exercises and pious practices in honor of the Holy Child. Her *Six Semaines à l'Ecole du Divin Enfant au Mois de l'Enfant Jésus* was a helpful and instructive guide to the devotion. Many other devotional booklets are credited to Gabrielle Fontaine as well as the establishment of the organization, *L'Oeuvre de l'Enfant Jesus,*[11] conducted by the Barnabite Fathers of Brussels for the purpose of spreading devotion to the Little King.

In 1905, the *Petite Revue de l'Enfant Jésus,* a periodical containing a wealth of devotional material, was published through the efforts of the enthusiastic devotee. It was through the untiring efforts of Gabrielle and the establishment of the shrine by her family that the French-speaking people became acquainted with the devotion and carried the message of the Little King to their far-flung missions.

The influence of these German and French contributors was also to be seen in the English. In 1894, the publishing house of Joseph Schaefer in New York City placed on the market a translation of Father Mayer's work by Father Herman Koneberg, O.S.B., entitled, *The Infant of Prague and its Veneration.* Apparently this was the first account in English in the United States and it enjoyed a large sale. Schaefer also published the original of Mayer's work in both German and French. In addition, he published a comprehensive but inexpensive booklet in English which ran to several editions, with at least seventy-five thousand copies having been printed in 1898. This booklet, *Devotion to the Miraculous Infant Jesus of Prague,* described in detail many of the favors received from the Holy Child, including some testimonials from America. Thus we may trace also a considerable influence of the Czech Mayer's account published in St. Louis in 1885.

A comparison of the literary contributions on the Infant during this time indicates the extent to which they are dependent on Emmerich's account. Monsignor Flische's work in the French language entitled: *Devotion à Jésus Enfant,* in the third edition of 1887, bears such similarity, although its own devotional aspect is expressed quite differently from the popular German account, *The Veneration of the Divine Infant Jesus,* by Father Rupert Mitz, published in 1796 in Neiderdorf, Germany. The work by Father Mitz is dependent upon another German account, a combination brief history and prayerbook, which appeared after Father Emmerich's *Pragerisches Gross und Klein.* Written by Countess Catherine Fugger-Boos, the work is entitled, *The Book of Kempten,* published in Kempten in 1761 and reprinted in 1791. Despite some confusion in its history, the devotional aspect is well developed and it is interesting to note the following:

"All who approach the miraculous image and pray to it with confidence receive support in danger, consolation in trouble, help in necessity, relief in anguish, light in spiritual darkness, waters of grace in dryness of soul, health in sickness and hope in despair. This miraculous image darts pure sparks of love from its lovely eyes and with smiling lips it offers us the richest blessings. Its beauty conquers all hearts.

"No colic is so painful, no fever so violent, no epidemic so dangerous, no peril so great, no loss so heavy, no passion so turbulent, no assault of Satan so furious, no pestilence so persistent, no tumor so malignant that it has not been helped. It frees captives from their bondage, delivers those condemned to death, brings hardened sinners to repentance, and bestows the blessings of children to the childless. In short, it has become all things to all."[12]

The preceding excerpt indicates that the writer was well acquainted with the miraculous events connected with the miraculous Image mostly from personal contact with the Carmelites in Prague.

A more original brief historical account entitled *Geshichte des gnadenreichen Prager Jezulein,* written most probably by a Carmelite nun and published in Luxemburg in 1895, shows its dependence on the original. The histories in the Italian rely heavily on Emmerich's version published in Trent in 1750. A popular account entitled *Il Santo Bambino miraculoso di Praga* was compiled by a Carmelite Father and published in Savona in 1898, while Mayer's Italian version appeared on the market in Venice in 1889. One of the more unique accounts is that of Father Jacob Sewcik, a well-known writer from the Lusitanian Serb group in Germany, who published his *Hnadowne Prazske Jezus-deecatko*[13] in Radworj in 1886. In 1925 a second edition was published by St. Hedwig's Printery, Niles, Illinois. In addition to its close similarity with the German histories, this account records some of the favors received in other lands.

Spanish contributions appeared in their periodicals, principally *El Messajero del Nino Jesus de Prague,* beginning in 1901, and *Ecos del Carmelo del Nino Jesus,* primarily for devotional purposes. It was not until 1924 that a more complete historical account, written by the Carmelite Father Doroteo de la S. Familia, entitled: *Historia Pro-*

digiosa del Milagroso Nino Jesus de Praga, was published in Barcelona.

While these few of the more important histories are reflections in the form of partial translations or abridged versions of Emmerich's account, the prayerbooks, which appeared simultaneously in nearly every language, following official ecclesiastical approval of the Confraternity of the Infant of Prague, show a marked degree of adaptability to the devotional needs of the time. Convinced that *Pragerisches Gross und Klein* fills a distinct need in our own time, the author is happy for the opportunity to present the work in its entirety. An observation of interest is that the publications are all dated near the end of the nineteenth century when the search was not solely for historical data concerning the beloved Infant of Prague, but also for some organized form, ecclesiastically approved and spiritually indulgenced for the benefit of devotees.

It was Cardinal Francis Schoenborn, Archbishop of Prague, who set in motion the beginnings of an organization which he called the *Sodality of the Infant Jesus of Prague.*[14] On January 18, 1895, he submitted the rules of the organization to Pope Leo XIII for approval. Perceiving the great need for humility, the outstanding lesson to be learned from the Holy Infancy, and the great spiritual benefits that would result from the devotion, Pope Leo XIII in his approval of the statutes of the Sodality on March 18, 1893, gave world-wide authorization for the organization.

The historical significance of this authorization becomes apparent when it is recalled that a similar organization, *The Family of the Infant Jesus* had already received ecclesiastical approval. Its origin is traced to Venerable Margaret of the Blessed Sacrament at the Carmel of Beaune. Its foundation was inspired by the Infant Jesus Himself in a revelation to the Carmelite nun, while the practical aspects of its formation were under the direction of the famed French theologian, Cardinal Bérulle. A study of the circumstances surrounding this positive sign of divine approval concerning the devotion to the Holy Infancy and the great theological understanding and mystical vision that accompanied it would prove spiritually beneficial. The great sanctity of this Carmelite nun was mirrored in her untiring efforts to make accessible to all the faithful, the treasures contained in devotion to the Holy Infancy, and spread to circles far wider than her immediate cloister the knowledge and love of the Child Jesus. In the interest of brevity, however, we must confine ourselves to a brief overview of the Family.

With nine members of the Community forming its nucleus, the organization was inaugurated on March 24, 1636. Following the death of the saintly Carmelite of Beaune, her spiritual director, Father Parisot, labored zealously in the cause of the Holy Childhood. The Family was approved and enriched with indulgences by Pope Alexander VII on January 24, 1661. After being suppressed during the time of the French Revolution, it was re-established by the Bishop of Dijon on December 26, 1821. Pope Pius IX enriched it by the papal bull of July 27, 1855 with new indulgences, and on December 24, 1855, proclaimed it the Archconfraternity of the Infant Jesus. The association exists today under the name of *Archiconfrèrie de l'Enfant Jésus.*

This *Archconfraternity of the Infant Jesus* (1636) must not be confused with the *Confraternity of the Infant of Prague,* founded in 1895. The similarities in background and motive of the two founders are noteworthy. Sister Margaret of the Blessed Sacrament and Father Cyril of the Mother of God were Carmelite contemporaries whose devotion to the Infant Jesus, some theologians point out, was the outward expression of a tradition that dates to the very founding of Carmel itself. Prague, through the efforts of Father Cyril became the Eastern center of the devotion, while Beaune through the revelation made to Sister Margaret became the western center for the spread of the love of the Holy Child.

A comparison of the rules for the *Confraternity of the Infant Jesus of Prague* (1895), and the regulations for the *Archconfraternity of the Infant Jesus* (1636) will show that the former emphasizes the external glory of the Infant King, while the latter stressed interior meditation on the Infant Jesus. Both, however, tend to follow the mysteries of the Holy Infancy.

The distinctive mission of the devotion to the Holy Child of Prague appears to be the most likely explanation for Pope Leo XIII's enthusiastic approval, and for his generosity in dispensing the rich indulgences from the spiritual treasury of the Church. It was inevitable that meditation on the Holy Infancy should result in bringing people to the feet of the Holy Child-the King. With the approval of the Sodality of the Infant of Prague as an important channel for spreading devotion from its headquarters at the Prague shine, France, Belgium and other countries, in an attempt to follow Prague's example, sought similar privileges for their shrines. With the rapid spread of the devotion throughout the world, many complications arose because of the numerous Sodalities and the varying indults. Because all countries endeavored to share proportionately in these indults, Pope St. Pius X unified all Sodalities under one set of rules. The saintly pontiff, foreseeing the important mission that the devotion could fulfill among children, issued on March 30, 1913 a decree giving perpetual Faculties to establish confraternities of the Holy Infant of Prague anywhere in the world.

With the unification of the Confraternities[15] and the clarification of their privileges established by this decision of Pope Pius X, the Sacred Congregation of the Council by decree of July 24, 1913, set forth a comprehensive list of requirements and regulations. Ten years later control of all Confraternities as decreed in an Apostolic letter of Pope St. Pius X was given over to the Discalced Carmelites. A review of these papal decrees is ample evidence of the earnest and persevering prayer of the Order of Carmel that the Infant Jesus might reign over the world, and that even as He holds the globe within the grasp of His tiny Hand, He might hold all Christendom within the bonds of charity. In addition to the decree of approval, already mentioned, Pope Benedict XV on November 24, 1920, granted an indult giving permission for a votive Mass of the Holy Name to be said wherever the Confraternity is canonically erected.

The Discalced Carmelites are, therefore, the official guardians of the devotion to the Holy Child of Prague and responsible for its apostolate. All other orders and congregations share their privileges by way of delegated power. Their jurisdiction extends to all national shrines as they appear in different countries. This does not create any difficulty in the establishment of a confraternity whenever a need for it is felt, and the consent of the local Ordinary is secured. On the contrary, a greater effectiveness and harmony is maintained through the centralization of control, and in addition to the Carmelite tradition, there is a practical advantage in this supervision of the devotion, namely that of securing the greatest measure of privileges for its members and devotees. It is unnecessary to detail here all the requirements for membership in such confraternities or to stress the spiritual benefits deriving from such membership since they are contained in numerous manuals prepared for devotional purposes. *Il Devoto del Santo Bambino Gesu de Praga,* a manual prepared by a Discalced Carmelite community of Arenzano in Italy, and published in 1920, and *Manuel de la Confrerie du Divin Enfant Jesus de Prague,* prepared by a Discalced Carmelite,

Father Theodore de Jesus, published in 1936, give eloquent testimony of Carmelite concern for the devotion. *The Spiritual Treasury of the Infant of Prague,* a complete manual and prayerbook in English, has been prepared by the author for publication and should be available within the coming year. Manuals and prayerbooks represent a literary contribution of a special kind and deserve mention as an important factor in the spread of the devotion.

It was not by accident that in the nineteenth and twentieth centuries the Great and Little One of Prague made His indelible mark on history. The after-effects of the neo-pagan era had maintained a firm hold on the human mind and the need for spiritual rejuvenation was effectively filled in the devotion to the Infant Jesus. In central Europe the "Away-from-Rome" movement had gathered such momentum that Bohemia was considered an outpost of "progressive" thinking, and Catholicism a symbol of reaction. The German *Kulturkampf* with its strong anti-Catholic tendencies had penetrated into all the neighboring countries, concentrating on those of the Czech Crown. The Church was forced to meet on all fronts with bitter antagonists in the form of liberalism, extreme nationalism, protestantism, freemasonry, "old" Catholicism, social democracy, and the already mentioned "Away-from-Rome" movement.[16]

It is general knowledge that the Catholic Church suffered much opposition from the successive crises that preceded and progressed into the twentieth century. The political scene during World War I from 1914 to 1918, with its complex and multiple causes, was only one lamentable survival of violent political ambitions vieing for precedence over one another. Under the guidance of the brilliant Popes of that time the Church was forced to ready herself for the challenge of a two-fold task: to recover from the wounds of the past, and to proceed in full vigor to meet the onslaught of new foes mobilizing against her.

The foregoing digression was made by way of explaining the semi-obscurity of the devotion to the Infant Jesus with relation to the era of general social unrest prevailing throughout the modern world. There were, however, some successes to record on the domestic scene. Through emigration channels from 1848 to 1913, devotion to the Infant Jesus of Prague reached the American continents and expanded with phenomenal success. When emigrants from Europe established themselves in their adopted lands, it was natural that certain mementos of the past would be among their most treasured possessions. Statues, miniatures, medals, prayer and picture cards of the Infant of Prague traveled with their owners into the new lands, and the demand for these devotionals reached tremendous proportions.

On October 28, 1918, Czechoslovakia was declared a republic and became one of several countries that emerged as a free nation from the disintegrating orbit of the Austro-Hungarian Empire. Following the rise to power of a dominantly Catholic People's Party in the 1930's, a relatively peaceful atmosphere was created in which the devout Czechoslovak people publicly expressed their reverent affection for the Infant of Prague. It must be acknowledged, however, that an outstanding factor in the revival of Czech devotion was the need to match their devotion against that of other nations. For it would indeed be unseemly to have the homeland of the Infant left behind in the far-reaching extent of the devotion.

The revival of the devotion to the Infant of Prague as directed by the Order of Carmel, following the approval and enthusiastic support of the Holy See, continued to thrive in all parts of the Catholic world. In 1925, on the occasion of the proclamation of the Feast of Christ the King[17] by Pope Pius XI, attention was sharply drawn to the special features of Divine Kingship as expressed in the image of the Great and Little One of Prague. Christians were given the timely reminder that man must attain to spiritual childhood, if he would attain to heaven. "Therefore let the rulers of nations not refuse to offer the public service of reverence and obedience to the power of Christ through themselves and through the people, if they wish truly, while preserving their authority, to advance and increase the fortunes of their country."[18] Coming at a time in the twentieth century, when exaggerated ideals of racial pride posed as nazism, and where spiritual values were obscured in the face of fascist secularism, perhaps the greatest lesson the modern world could learn from its experience with false ideologies is the directive, "Render to Caesar the things that are Caesar's and to God the things that are God's."[19] And to those who seriously seek to apply the words of wisdom to the culture, politics and problems of their day there is the heartening promise, *"The more you will honor Me, the more I will bless you."*

Realizing this it is understandable that the Great and Little One of Prague should be dramatically brought to the fore in the spiritual, cultural, artistic, and devotional literary work of the time, and achieve a focal point of tremendous importance on the domestic scene as well as abroad.

The Infant of Prague became a beloved theme in the world of art and literature. There is a warmth in tone and beauty in form that is easily discernible in the expression of great artists, writers, and poets in their approach to the Infant. The great Czech poet, Julius Zeyer expressed his love for the Infant on many occasions and in many works, the most outstanding of which is his *Marianska Zahrada.* Strangely enough, his love for Prague's Little King was kindled in France by his choice of a vacation site. The essays of Jiri Karasek Lvovic reflect the religious sentiments of the Czech people in their legends and folklore,[20] surrounding the Infant more in the national spirit than in the devotional one.

Zdenka Braunerova[21] expressed in her artistic representations of the Infant her own tender regard for the Little King, and awakened a religious consciousness in the Prague of her day. Her work was an expression of her own vibrant spiritual living, unique in the liberal society of the time. Catholic leaders were gratified to enlist her moral courage in exposing the neo-pagan tendencies so much in evidence in this period of such religious and political significance. Her death in 1935 was mourned as a great loss to cultural Prague.

Henri Bordeaux,[22] distinguished novelist of the French Academy, was another champion of the devotion to the Infant, deriving his inspiration from his mother's great personal devotion which she expressed in her many pilgrimages to the shrine of the Infant in Prague. In his literary work he refers only indirectly to the Infant, despite his personal enthusiasm for the devotion. In this regard he may be compared with Edith Stein, Jewish convert, and German philsopher, better known as Sister Benedicta of the Carmel at Cologne, who was wholly absorbed in her dedication to the Infant. At Echt in Holland she found a brief refuge following her expulsion from Cologne by the Nazis. On August 2, 1942 she was herded with other "non-Aryan" members of Dutch religious communities to the gas chambers of Auschwitz. Confiding herself and her companions to her dear "Holy Child of Prague" she went to her death holding in her hand the picture of her beloved Little King. Her literary contributions on the Infant are scattered. Her life itself, with its unlimited dedication and mystical communication with the Infant, represents perhaps the best "poem" ever written about the Infant of Prague.

In contemporary fiction, a similar heroism is to

be found in Gertrud von Le Fort's *Song at the Scaffold.*[23] In this novelette the courage of sixteen Carmelites of Paris is portrayed as they approach the guillotine during the Reign of Terror. A novice, Blanche La Force, tempted against her vocation, drops the image of the Infant King as she hears the wild strains of the *Carmagnole* beyond her convent walls, and leaves the cloister to join the revolutionist "liberators." When the nuns make an abortive effort to transport their "Infant King of Glory" out of Paris into the relative safety of the convent in Compiegne, an inventory of the Infant's wardrobe is seized and the words "Mantle of the Crown" are distorted to mean garments intended for the little Dauphin. The accusation leads the Carmelite martyrs to their doom, and gives Blanche the courage to join them in their song at the scaffold. Against the historic background of the French revolution devotion and dedication to the Infant are set in bold relief as an unfailing source of strength and courage in time of need.

Another inspiring example of this is the case of Dr. Alfred Fuchs (1892-1942).[24] A convert from Judaism, talented journalist and literary genius, Fuchs numbers many poems, essays and hymns to the Infant of Prague among his prodigious writings. His works encompassing books and periodicals are so numerous as to defy measure. He and his wife directed their talents to spreading the ideals of "my Little King," as he affectionately termed the Image. An extraordinarily eloquent speaker, he was constantly in demand at the various political and cultural gatherings and congresses for which Prague was famous. Following his arrest by the Nazis, he was tortured, bound with his hands behind his back, drenched with water and left to freeze to death outside the barracks of the infamous camp at Dachau. It must be said that Fuchs appears to be one of the greatest in the Czech literary world. His knowledge of many languages and his devotion to the Infant was a moving factor in the spread of the devotion at home and abroad. His last words were fittingly a supplication to his Little King: "My dear Infant of Prague, bless and protect me!"[25]

The greatest literary achievement in connection with the Infant of Prague must be credited to Paul Claudel, whose influence reached to the far corners of the earth and penetrated all literary circles. Claudel "was like a volcano of creativity, belching forth masterpieces, flowing over all other fields, warming his time with the heat of his passion and lighting it with his vision."[26] That Claudel's devotion to the Infant was not merely artistic, but very deeply and personally devout, helps one to an understanding of his vision and the importance and extent of his spiritualizing influence. Nevertheless, even in such a brief review as this, mention must be made of the literary beauty of his poem, *l'Enfant Jésus de Prague,* so touching and beautiful in its tone, form, content, and expression. It was written when his diplomatic career had led him to Prague and to the regally robed Child King. Overwhelmed by sentiments of gratitude for his conversion in the days of his youth, he was inspired to write his beautiful poem. In the moving and impressive brief autobiographical essay, *Ma Conversion,* Claudel writes of his experience on Christmas Day, 1886 at Notre Dame Cathedral in Paris. He describes his state of despair and reminisces, "It was then that the event took place which revolutionized my whole life. . . . I was overcome with a sudden and overwhelming sense of the innocence and eternal infancy of God—an inexpressible revelation."[27] It was this recollection that prompted him, as he knelt before the Image of the Holy Child, to express his deep sentiments for the Little King. Although his *l'Enfant Jésus de Prague* was published originally in a volume of religious poetry called *Corona Benignitatis Anni Dei*[28] in 1915, it was not until 1927 that his poem exerted its real influence on the history of the Infant.

At this time the new ambassador to the United States was asked by the editor of *Forum* to select one of his poems as a subject for a national contest. Paul Claudel selected his beloved *l'Enfant Jésus de Prague.* The attention of all America was focused on the Infant of Prague when the January issue of *Forum* in 1928 announced that one thousand manuscripts had been received as contest material.[29] The choice of the Infant as the subject and the unusual response to the contest emphasized the popularity of the Holy Child to the puzzlement of some critics in liberal circles. The many beautiful English translations, especially that of Molly Anderson Haley of Richmond Hill, first prize winner in the contest, were not only valuable literary contributions, but expressive tributes to the Infant of Prague and the poet Paul Claudel. During the Holy Year of 1950, Claudel's poem once again drew the attention of the world to the Infant of Prague. Fellow pilgrims, members of the Parisian *Théatre Herbertót,* interpreted many of Claudel's poems during their audience with the Holy Father, Pope Pius XII. On April 29, 1950, the poet-diplomat chose for his own reading the poem "l'Enfant Jésus de Prague." He received a resounding ovation from the colorful audience of diplomats, Cardinals, Vatican officials, artists and writers, and extraordinary praise from the Holy Father himself. News commentators, secular and ecclesiastical newspapers were unanimous in their generous praise of the poem and its author.

Claudel's influence on the literary works of this time is particularly noteworthy in the writings of Maurice Martin du Gard and the American contemporary poet, Father Charles J. Dvorák, pastor of Holy Angels Church, Childress, Texas, whose enthusiasm kept pace with his art. The essays of Josef Simanek of Prague also bear the stamp of Claudel's influence. Among his most enthusiastic followers were the Benedictine Fathers of St. Procopius Church, Chicago. Father Josef Chvatal, who died in 1958, included Claudel's poem in his devotional material. More organized in form are the literary contributions of Father Augustine Studeny (1887-1956) whose English Novena booklet published in Chicago in 1948, contains much original material, including his *Hymn* to the Infant.

At the time of Claudel's death, Father Studeny

wrote of his admiration for the poet and his work. These articles appeared in many Czech and English newspapers. The greatest single contribution of these Benedictines was the thirty-six-hundred-word syndicated article on the Infant of Prague prepared for the 1953 supplement of the Catholic Encyclopedia. The wave of enthusiasm for the Infant of Prague which swept through the literary circles of this time was utilized well by these American priests of Czech descent for devotional purposes.

Among many booklets published in the United States at this time, one might be singled out as excellent. A short, popular historical account with vivid narrative in modern style is *The Infant King* by Audrey May Meyer, published by the Benedictines of St. Meinrad, Indiana, in 1951. Its author is to be commended for her distinctive understanding of the proper mission of the devotion, with its stress on the Kingship of the Holy Child of Prague.

Claudel's publicity for the Infant of Prague was re-echoed by the Discalced Carmelites of Arenzano, Italy, who continued to publish worth-while material in their monthly periodical, *Il Messagero de S. Bambino Gesu di Praga,* which began publication in 1905. From their literary efforts the devotion was rapidly developed, and the shrine at Arenzano became world-famous. The complete dedication of these Carmelites is to be found in their idea of celebrating the Coronation of the Holy Child of Prague. Thus the solemn celebration, in fact a ceremonial coronation of a King, helped the devotees to grasp the concept of the Kingship of the Holy Child. With the approval of the Holy See the event took place on February 24, 1924. The ceremony was so effectively and impressively carried out that the shrine was raised to the rank of a Minor Basilica on May 6, 1928, the only one in the world dedicated to the Infant of Prague at the present time. These zealous promoters utilized every means possible to further the devotion.

All these events, together with the publicity aroused by Claudel and the devotional progress being made in other countries, exerted a great influence on the domestic scene in Prague. On the occasion of the tercentenary commemorating the presentation of the miraculous Image to the Discalced Carmelites[30] in Prague by Princess Polyxena in 1628, the Father General of the Order requested from the Holy See indulgences to be made available to people all over the world. Celebrated with great solemnity the event (on April 5, 1928) moved the Czechoslovak people to a deep awareness of the great national and spiritual treasure they possessed. Present were high state and ecclesiastical officials. The famous writer and historian, Most Reverend Antonin Podlaha, Auxiliary Bishop of Prague, pontificated, attended by the General of the Order of Crosiers, the Most Reverend Josef Vlasak. In his inspirational sermon, the Right Reverend Method Zavoral, Abbot of the Premonstratensians of Prague, recalled the historic promise that in honoring the Infant of Prague the whole Czech nation could expect rich benefits. The commemoration brought about a better understanding of the providential mission of the Holy Child - the King.

The golden era of the devotion appears to coincide with the consecration of Charles Kaspar, bishop of Hradec Králové, as Archbishop of Prague. Inspired by the "little way" of St. Therese of Lisieux, he endeavored to imitate it in his own saintly apostolate. His devotion to the Infant was displayed on many occasions. In January, 1933 he wrote a pastoral letter[31] in which he advocated that devotion to the Infant should become the center of all spiritual life in Czechoslovakia. Under the Cardinal's interested guidance, devotional activities throughout the nation were centered in the Sodality of the Infant Jesus of Prague. With the publication of *Od Prazskeho Jezulatka* (From the Infant Jesus of Prague) the influence of this organization reached international proportions. The foreword of the initial issue urged readers to seek refuge in all their needs in the Infant of Prague. *Osservatore Romano,* the Vatican daily, praised the Knights of Malta who sponsored the quarterly for a "commendable undertaking in these times of 'World Days' and 'Youth Days' wherein no thought is given to the most beautiful example of youth, namely the Christ Child Himself." It stated further: "Its circulation will foster this pleasing devotion to the Infant Jesus of Prague, who is honored everywhere in the world, and with Whom are associated so many wonders, both spiritual and temporal."[32] Before the publication had an adequate opportunity to establish itself, it was forced out of circulation in 1938 by the ban on the free press imposed during the Nazi occupation.

World attention was[33] again focused on the Infant of Prague in June 1935 when the National Catholic Congress was held in Prague and used the Church of Our Lady of Victory for its devotional sessions. The universal theme of the Congress was due to the emphasis of Pope Pius XI on Christ—the King, but its practical aspect was centered about the Infant of Prague as a King.

The anniversary celebration of the first historical coronation,[34] April 19, 1936, marked another occasion which drew attention to the concept of the Holy Child - the King. Aware of the civil war raging in Spain, and exhorted by Cardinal Kaspar in a pastoral letter to "make novenas for tortured war-torn Spain, whence this miraculous Image came to us,"[35] few of the participants could foresee how desperately their own nation would need the special help of the Infant.

Cardinal Kaspar's personal and episcopal correspondence is indicative of his interest in promoting this devotion. His *imprimatur* appears in a number of devotional booklets and he granted ecclesiastical approval for the publication of the 1940 Symposium, *Prazske Jezulatko,* edited by Vladimir Zikes of Prague, who presented the history, legends, devotional expansion, with hymns and prayers honoring the Infant. In symposium style, this material, although concise, is richly informative and generously illustrated. The Cardinal granted permission to historians to use the monastery archives and library of the Carmelite Sisters in Prague. Under his patronage many international organizations held their conventions in Prague, with the Shrine of the Infant the center of their program.

Through the efforts of Father John Font Girald,[37] editor of *Espero Katolike,* the international monthly of the Esperantists, publicity about the Infant of Prague stimulated interest in the devotion. The contest sponsored by the Esperantists in 1935 on the theme, "How the Infant Jesus of Prague Is Honored Abroad,"[38] received international response, with the five winning essays coming from India, Trinidad, Belgium, Spain, and Poland. Through the widely distributed writings of Spanish Esperantists, Japan, China, India, and other countries in the Far East became acquainted for the first time with Father Cyril's *Prayer to the Infant,* printed in *Esperanto* on holy cards featuring the Infant. The Infant of Prague was invoked by Esperantist Congresses and His image displayed on the banner of their international organization.

There is no doubt that the contact between these international organizations and Prague helped considerably in keeping the Infant before the public, and thus effectively spread devotion to other continents. The International Union of Catholic Esperantists is especially to be commended for its effort in utilizing every possible means of communication to "internationalize" the Infant of Prague. The same is true of the International Movement of Catholic Students with its general secretariet in Fribourg, Switzerland. The efforts of this organization have been even more successful since its national branch in Prague numbered among its members such outstanding personalities as Dr. Fuchs, Antonin Sorm, Bela Dlouhá, the Franciscan Father, John E. Urban, Antonin Eltshkner, Auxiliary Bishop of Prague, Father John Filip, Father John Strakos, Monsignor Josef Beran, present Archbishop of Prague, Professor Josef Hlouch, Bishop of Ceske Budejovice, and the priests of the Knights of Malta.

The efforts of the various religious congregations of sisters, particularly the School Sisters of the Third Order of St. Francis in Prague, the Ursulines in Prague, and the Dominican Sisters in Olomouc, to mention a few, were very helpful in establishing a tradition of dedicating their academic endeavors in honor of the Infant. Many booklets, pamphlets, pictures and prayer cards were printed under their auspices. *Milostne Prazke Jezulatko* (The Miraculous Infant Jesus of Prague) by Frank X. Toupalik is especially noteworthy. It is a popular account of the story of the Infant and contains material on the devotion not derived from Emmerich's account.

The intensified drive to spread the apostolate of the Infant was accompanied by an attempt to reappraise the Baroque era and to remove the unjustified term of "darkness" which writers and historians had unfortunately applied to this period. Josef Pekar, the Jesuit Father, Blazej Rácek, Bohdan Chudoba, Zdenek Wirth, Alzbeta Birnbaumova and other historians, aided in their efforts by art critics and literary analysts such as Josef Vasica and

Arne Novak, opened the door to a new admiration and appreciation of the Baroque. When Baroque culture groups met at a Congress in Prague in 1938, their critique of Baroque art was decidedly different from that issued in former years. The majority of those in attendance considered devotion to the Infant the barometer of Baroque culture, the change in attitude being due primarily to the world-wide attention focused on the Infant and the research that had followed it.

As a consequence of the re-evaluation of the Baroque, theologians proceeded to look more closely into the spiritual foundation of the devotion for a clearer understanding. Taking the initiative were the Dominican Fathers in Olomouc under the able direction of their talented writer and orator, Father Silvester M. Braito. Contained in their monthly review, *Nahlubinu,* are many items on the Infant. The direction of this cultural movement attracted many artists who offered their talents in the service of the Little King. Outstanding are the woodcarvings of Father Arnost Hrabal.[39]

The encouragement given to the devotion by the active sponsorship of Cardinal Kaspar was also to be one of the main interests of his successor, Josef Beran, Archbishop of Prague. While a professor at St. Anne's from 1925 to 1933, and afterwards as rector of the Major Theological Seminary in Prague, Monsignor Beran laid a firm foundation for this apostolate among the future teachers and priests of the Archdiocese. As they had been urged to do some years earlier, the residents of Prague terrorized by the German Gestapo looked for refuge in the Infant. The Church of Our Lady of Victory was crowded to capacity with daily worshippers. Booklets of devotion were not available in quantities sufficient to meet the popular demand.

Monsignor Josef Beran, exiled for devotion to the Church in the time of its Nazi persecutors, led the vanguard of the devotion. On the first day of his return from the concentration camp of Dachau, where he had been interned from 1942 to 1945, he visited the shrine of the Infant of Prague. He offered his first Mass of thanksgiving at the shrine, and continued to foster devotion after being raised to the archbishopric. The 1948 second edition of the Zikes publication of the devotion contains his foreword, and numerous booklets and picture cards bear his *imprimatur*. He blessed many statues which were sent to foreign lands and mission territories. Diplomatic relations between Czechoslovakia and the countries of South America were considerably strengthened by these expressions of appreciation for the Infant, especially in those critical times when mutual trust among nations was so little in evidence.

In their tradition of music, the Czech people can point with pride to the spiritual quality of their songs. Their folk tunes are so prayerful in content that they might well be classified as hymns. Their Christmas music, notably that of the Jesuit Fredrich Bridel, abounds in tender lines to the Holy Child of Prague. The artistic simplicity of some of the more popular music dedicated to the Infant follows closely in this tradition. In the Czech version of Emmerich's *Prazske Welike y Male* of 1749, the style is dominantly nationalistic. An outstanding composer of this type of music was Dr. Jaroslav Macha of Prague, whose reputation had been established as early as 1895 with the publication of his "Lamb of God." More popularly esteemed, however, was his "Prayer to the Infant Jesus of Prague"[40] composed during the time of the Nazi oppression. The lyrics borrowed from A. Creova completed a combination which proved expressive of the nation's feelings at their liberation from Nazi occupation in May, 1945. The composition was so enthusiastically received that it may be justifiably termed the spiritual if not the national anthem of the Czech people. More majestic in tone and theme was the *Oratorio*[41] presented at a pontifical High Mass offered by Archbishop Beran in Prague on April 5, 1948. This composition with lyrics by Nina Svobodova and music by Jilji Walter, organist at Our Lady of Victory, attracted considerable attention from music critics and the public, since members of the National Theatre in Prague had been invited to perform the scores written for orchestra as well as choir and solo voices. In the hope that the Oratorio might be selected for use during the celebration of the Holy Year in 1950, the composer submitted his work to the Vatican, receiving high praise from Maestro Perosi. It is unfortunate that this composition did not reach a greater circulation abroad. Limited to Prague with its present political atmosphere, it has, temporarily at least, been forced into oblivion.

Following the communist *coup-d-état* in February, 1948, the calvary of the Catholic Church in Czechoslovakia began anew. Archbishop Beran was placed under house arrest and silenced on June 19, 1949. In 1948, he had officially changed the name of the Church of Our Lady of Victory to that of "Our Lady of the Infant Jesus of Prague," and transferred its administration to the priests of the Order of Comforters of the Sacred Heart. No reason had been given for the change. Speculation was that the administrator, Prior Bobe, had left much to be desired in his custodianship during the war years. The communists ignored the official ecclesiastical change and appointed Father Picha of the Maltese Knights and Father Charles Horky as custodians of the shrine, with all administrative detail to be kept in control of a state bureau for ecclesiastical affairs, which is the situation at the present time. The farce of Archbishop Beran's "deposition" occurred on March 10, 1951.

It would be a grave mistake to assume that during this time of cultural vandalism and religious persecution in Czechoslovakia, devotion to the Infant had ceased to exist. Despite the suppressive measures imposed by state censorship, devotion to the Infant was strengthened by those very restrictions, and even the oppressors realized that it was not to be crushed. As always, when communists are forced to a concession, they utilize it as a propaganda tool.

In their attempts to disseminate their ideology

abroad, the Czechoslovak communists have capitalized on the national Patron. In the profusely illustrated English translation of the Czech book, *Unto the Glory of God,*[42] published by Caritas in Prague, 1955, is to be found an interesting article, "The Infant Jesus of Prague," admitting the flourishing state of the devotion. Whatever their intention in attemping to exploit the devotion the amazing fact remains that the communists were forced to capitulate to the influence of the miraculous statue and the devotion. It is a known fact that they tried by every means to end this "popish superstition" but could not afford to antagonize a popular reaction, choosing instead to tolerate it. So today, officials of the powerful Ministry of Education must look from their windows upon the Shrine of the Infant where people with the devotion still firmly rooted in their hearts come to "liberate" themselves at least internally from the nonsense and contradictions of communist education. The gratifying fact remains that the Holy Child of Prague continues behind the Iron Curtain His magnificent role of blessing all the faithful who have never renounced their loyalty to the Church of Silence. The intensified devotion abroad appears as a compensation for the honor officially but temporarily denied Him in His enslaved homeland.

Typical of their propaganda methods is an attractive twelve-page brochure bearing the *"imprimatur"* of Antonius Stehlik under date of November 5, 1956. Anonymously written in French, this is a communist publication designed to use the image of the Infant to divert the attention of the free world from the real state of religious affairs in Czechoslovakia. We quote briefly from one of its closing paragraphs:

> Every day three priests offer divine service in this church (Our Lady of Victory) in the presence of men of the faithful. There is no time from morning till night when one cannot see kneeling before the altar some person venerating the Little Infant Jesus. They come from Prague, from other places in Bohemia, from Moravia, from Slovakia. Strangers come there when they attend the international congresses frequently organized in Prague. Just this year a numerous delegation of sportsmen came from Brazil on April 4, 1956, to pray to the Little Infant; likewise on July 3, there came a delegation of Vietnamese Catholics.[43]

Even from communist propaganda some good may come. *Caritas* in Prague continues to supply the foreign market and perhaps even the homeland with a collection of sixteen full-color pictures, originally printed by the publisher, Zikes. They represent in picture form the history of the Infant in His historical robes. Except for Latin captions, there is no text. This publication may well prove an inspiration to artists abroad to interpret the Infant's message in new artistic creations. The jacket design of this book is one example. The young artist, John Leo Baker of Pittsburgh, depicts in an original interpretation the Infant of Prague as the King of Nations and the Universe, using the historical representation of the Infant in its Chinese robes.

Another recent variant of the Infant of Prague

has been created by Suzanne Silvercruys Stevenson.[44] Her interpretation of the Infant is carved of white linden wood, standing two and a half feet high. An American by choice since 1922, Mme. Silvercruys is a sculptor of international repute, the daughter of the late Baron Silvercruys, former President of the Supreme Court of Belgium, and a sister of the present Baron Silvercruys, Belgian Ambassador to the United States. Fordham University in New York sponsored the exhibition of liturgical art created by this gifted artist in 1941. A popular lecturer, she has delighted American audiences speaking on the subject of "Peace of Mind through Artistic Endeavors," and sketching a portrait of some member of her audience as she speaks in a humorous, philsophical and inspiring way. Her image of the Infant of Prague adorns St. Philip's Church in Warrendale, Connecticut.

There is a wide variation in the facial appearance of the statues and statuettes produced abroad. Czech artists have endeavored to keep a close similarity with the original, while the work of American artists such as Suzanne Silvercruys, reveals their distinctive interpretations. Certain European countries have been influenced in their variations by the "Roi de Gloire" of France and Belgium. The Italian and Spanish maintain for the most part an adequate similarity to the original.

Medals of recent date honoring the Infant are not so elaborate as those made by the Czech artists, Stanek, Karnet, or Kysely of Prague. Some show a greater trend toward simplicity, depicting the figure of the Infant with an inscription or the text of the "Promise" and others appear as "mutes" without any inscription.[45] Regardless of their differences, these devotionals represent in an artistic way the practical application of the knowledge gained from different literary contributions about the Infant derived in whole or part from Emmerich's account. Only when an idea is fully comprehended can it be faithfully reflected in an artistic representation. It is the hope of the author that this first English version of *Pragerisches Gross und Klein* will increase artistic aspirations and result in a renewed interest faithfully in keeping with the original, thus curtailing the production of some of the monstrous representations which lack not only the esthetic sense but any relation to the concept supposed to be embodied in it. A brief look at the number and variety of the devotional media available throughout the world gives indication of the popularity of the Infant of Prague, but more than that, it gives evidence of the fact that the Great and Little One of Prague "holds the whole world in His hands."

In view of the world-wide popularity of the Infant of Prague, it is not at all surprising to find a poem dedicated to Him among the "Flowers for Faith and Friendship" published by James J. Metcalfe under the title *Garden in My Heart.*[46] In this slender volume one of America's best loved contemporary poets displays a deep understanding of the day-to-day joys and tribulations that mark the Christian path of life. Like his popular and widely syndicated *Poem Portraits,* the Garden poems reveal rich spiritual value, and apply to all who believe in God, regardless of their creed. With something akin to the talent of John Bannister Tabb, the Civil War priest-poet, Metcalfe shows a talent for compressing great religious truth within simple devotional lines that easily reach the hearts of the millions of men who recognize the Divine Child as the King of Heaven and earth. His poetic prayer to the Infant follows:

O INFANT JESUS OF PRAGUE

O Infant Jesus, sweet and mild . . . We lift our eyes to You . . . O holy little King of Prague . . . We promise to be true . . . You rule the land and sea . . . While in Your honor You hold the world . . . And all its destiny . . . You give Your blessings to the ones . . . Who honor You today . . . As surely as Your Heart is grieved . . . By those who go astray . . . O gently little Majesty . . . We bow before Your feet . . . While humbly we entreat . . . O Infant Jesus, let us share . . . The blessings You bestow . . . That we may tell Your miracles . . . For everyone to know.[47]

The foregoing brief review of the literary, artistic, and religious representations of the Great and Little One of Prague testifies to a devotion that may be found in all parts of the world as detailed in an earlier work, *The Infant of Prague*.

While these esthetic values have been established they would be pointless without a consideration of the practical aspect of this devotion as evidenced by the unmatched demand for devotionals honoring the Great and Little One. The consequent sales volume of these devotionals attests to the real devotion of millions of devotees who have apparently understood the correlation between honoring and blessing, by taking literally the promise: "The more you honor Me, the more I will bless you."

It is hoped that the important message "To restore all things in Christ" has been grasped, and that having understood through Bethlehem the messianic mission of littleness, His followers will come, with the Magi, to an understanding of the important concept of greatness as embodied in Christ the King.

EPILOGUE

Devotion is the external expression of the human mind and heart directed to its ultimate object. Religious devotion goes beyond this to a spiritual concentration of the mind and heart on a sacred symbol as a medium of divine power, help and protection. The relationship of man to God is based on the recognition of this principle and only insofar as man manifests his love for his King may he be said to offer true worship.

Empirical or communicated knowledge about such a medium impels one to the practice of such devotion whenever he becomes cognizant of needs beyond his own powers to satisfy. The history of the miraculous statue of the Infant of Prague abounds in such experience and manifests itself as a tremendous source of consolation. The devotion that followed upon the acceptance of the historic promise of the Infant to bless those who honor Him was in some way embodied in the concept of the Great and Little One. It must ever be borne in mind that the miraculous image is but the symbol of a spiritual principle of greatness and littleness. The essence of the devotion is the awesome realization of the Majesty and Omnipotence of God, with the certitude that all things are possible to Him, yet in the irresistible appeal of His "Littleness" all timidity in approaching Him is lost, and great and trifling problems are confidently entrusted to His care. From this one learns that littleness here is a prerequisite for greatness in eternity.

With a proper understanding of the devotion, the historic role of the image takes on richer significance and the veneration afforded it through the centuries and throughout the world assumes a deeper meaning. True, there is an emotional appeal, but fundamentally it is on a sound theological basis that the intellectual acceptance of the Great and Little One rests.

The patronages under which the Great and Little One is invoked are many. He has become the Master of Vocations, being supplicated by almost every religious order and congregation for an increase of worthy members. Since the first recorded favor was that of reassurance of his religious vocation for Father Cyril of the Mother of God, it is not surprising to find this devotion among religious, nor is it presumptuous to expect that the Little King would take special care of those whose prime concern is to spread His glory.

Known as the Protector of Families, His image is lovingly enshrined in millions of homes, and it is thus in honoring Him that the blessing of a good home provides the proper spiritual atmosphere where the children of God may "advance in wisdom, age, and grace before God and men."

Perhaps the most affectionate expression of love for the "Little King" is to be found in hospitals, orphanages, and other institutions where God's exceptional children honor in their own little way the Infant of Prague. "Suffer the little children to come to Me" is the directive of the Saviour, and it is to these little ones that His graces are showered in abundance.

Financial difficulties confided to the provident care of the Little King have been successfully resolved in so many instances that He is invoked under the title of Good Financier. Patron of Good Health and Safeguard of Reputations are two more of the patronages of the Infant. Mentioned here are only a few of the many patronages under which the Great and Little One is invoked, for there is help and consolation to be found at the feet of the Little King in any trial or suffering. None who seek His help will do so in vain, because "all power in heaven and earth" was given Him.

Since the blessing of God is proportionate to the degree of worship afforded Him, it can be readily seen that the spread of His glory is a requisite for real devotion to the Infant - the King. The whole world, subject to His sovereignty, belongs to Him. This is impressively symbolized in the miraculous Image which depicts the Little King clasping the globe in His left hand while blessing it with His right. It would seem that Divine Providence utilizes this very appropriate symbol of the Little King, so acceptable and understandable to all peoples, to advance the apostolate of the Kingdom of God.

In an earlier work, *THE INFANT OF PRAGUE,* the wide-spread scope of the devotion to the Infant was given extensive treatment, and it is not our purpose to detail it here. However, it must be mentioned that America is a land where the devotion is deep-rooted and a continent comparable to Europe in honoring the Little King of Prague. From such European centers as Czechoslovakia, Belgium, France, Italy and Spain, the devotion was brought to America.

The reason for the speedy development of the devotion lies in the fact that immigrants to the Americas and Canada brought their national religion and culture with them in the hope of pursuing happiness in a free land, with its promising outlook for economic prosperity.

Foremost among these immigrants were the Czechs who brought with them the Devotion as an integral part of their national heritage. So we find that the statue of the Infant Jesus of Prague was enthroned for public veneration as early as 1854 in the Church of St. John Nepomucene in St. Louis, Missouri.

Following their tradition of devotion to the Holy Infancy, the Carmelites of both branches were greatly instrumental in acquainting the American people with the devotion through the veneration of the Image in all their monasteries. No less devoted to the cause of the Infant were the secular Czech priests who fostered the devotion at St. Wenceslaus, one of the oldest churches in Chicago, and their contemporaries, the Czech Benedictines of St. Procopius, Chicago, were equally zealous. In New York, the Redemptorist Fathers established the devotion as a means of contact and missionary work among the Czech immigrants, and as early as 1887 the Sisters of the Poor of St. Francis had placed statues in St. Joseph Hospital for Incurables where they served as solace and spiritual comfort.

An important factor in the general acceptance of the statue and the devotion in this land, which is predominantly protestant, is that the difficulty arising from the veneration of the saints and their images is obviated in the case of the miraculous statue, because it is a representation of the Son of God Himself.

The Infant enshrined in almost every Catholic church, convent, monastery, and institution of every type and a beloved member of millions of families is a great public testimonial to the dedication of the American people to the Great and Little One of Prague.

It is the earnest hope of the author that the thoughtful consideration of the glorious history of the Great and Little One of Prague will result in a spread of this devotion, so that there will be a steady increase in the number of those who gather near His throne to participate in the fulfillment of His solemn promise; "The more you honor Me, the more I will bless you."

REFERENCES

TABLE OF ABBREVIATIONS

AAS . . . . Acta Apostolicae Sedis
AER . . . . The American Ecclesiastical Review
ES . . . . Enchiridion Symbolorum (Denziger)
IPQ . . . . Periodical of Od Prazského Jezulátka (Prague)
PR . . . . Petite Revue de L'Enfant Jesus (published Brussels)

PART I

CHAPTER 1. The Holy Child in Art

1. Patrick J. Temple, *Pattern Divine* or Our Lord's Hidden Li (St. Louis: Herder) 149-56, 327-34, *cfr.* "Jesus Grew in Wisdom, AER 103 (1940) 92-93. *cfr.* Ferd. Prat. *Jesus Christ, His Life, His Teaching and His Work* (trans. by John J. Heenan, 2 vols. Milwaukee: 1950) 110-40; *cfr.* Paul Bernardi, *The Divine Child* (Th. St. Washington, D. C. 1952) 174-5; *cfr.* Stanley B. James, "Glory hidden in Humility," *The Ave Maria* 65 (1947) 423-25).
2. Henry Van Dyke "The Childhood of Jesus," *Harper's New Monthly Magazine,* 87 (1893) 723-30.
3. This difference between Galilee and Judea results not only from geographical reasons but also from their traditions.
4. Detailed knowledge of Holy Scriptures was required as an integral part of education.
5. *PR* 29 (1933) 162: *cfr.* Henry Jenner, *Christ in Art* (New York: 1923), 1-17.
6. *Mary Mother of God.* (Chicago: 1950) 9-29; *cfr.* Jacques Maritain *Creative Intuition in Art and Poetry.* (New York: 1955).
7. Bertola, "Il culto di Gesu Bambino nell' arte cristians de primi secoli," *Il Messaggero* 50:12 (1954) 6-7.
8. Walter Lowrie, *Art in the Early Church* (New York: 1947) 81-82.
9. Bertola, *Op. cit.,* 7.
10. *Ibid.*

11. Giovanni B. de Rossi, *La Roma sotterranes cristiana,* 3 vols. plates and atlas. (Rome: 1864-77, a fourth volume was prepared by Orazio Marucchio.).

12. A. G. Radcliffe, *Schools and Masters of Painting.* (New York: 1897), 17 . . . most of these so-called portraits are, however, considered to have been executed by a monk named Luca who flourished about the eleventh century. . . . Beneath this image of the Mother of God in the Borghese Chapel in St. Mary Major Basilica, Pius XII offered his first Mass. He made a special visit to the Chapel on the day he solemnly opened the Marian year, December 8, 1953; on November 1, 1954 the Salus Populi Romani was crowned with a diadem of twelve stars.

13. *Perpetual Help,* 3 (1953), 407-9.

14. "Proud Byzantium's Christian Treasure," *Life* (June, 1951). *cfr. Register* (July 17, 1951).

15. Cyril G. E. Bunt, *A History of Russian Art.* (London and New York: 1946) *cfr.* David Talbot Rice, *Russian Icons.* (London and New York: 1947) 11, *cfr.* Clem M. Henze, *Mater de Perpetuo Succursu* (Bonn am Rheim: 1926) 109-111.

16. "The Oldest Madonna," *Time,* (May 16, 1955), 88.

17. A. G. Radcliffe, *Op. cit.,* 29.

18. *Ibid.*

19. "The Story of Christ," *Life* (December 27, 1948) 20 pages of Giotto's Paintings in color.

20. Andre Leclerc, *Fra Angelico* (New York) 8.

21. National Gallery of Art, *Book of Illustrations.* (Washington, D. C., 1948).

22. *Masterpieces,* 1 (1950) 36; *cfr.* Cynthia Pearl Maus, *The World's Great Madonnas* (New York: 1947) 26-8.

23. *A. Berenson Anthology cfr. 25th Art News Annual,* 25 (1956) 36 *cfr.* Thomas Bodwin, *The Virgin and Child* (London-New York: 1949) 18.

24. "Tintoretto's Story of Christ," *Life* (December 24, 1951) 20 pages in color.

25. Famous monastery of Strahov in Prague was taken by Communists, 1950, and its gallery is now a state museum; *cfr.* George Noel, *Albert Durer* (Paris: 1950), 21.

26. Maurice Serullaz, *El Greco,* (Paris: Vendome: 1947); G. G. Coulton, *Art and the Reformation* (New York: 1928).

27. E. V. Tristram, *English Medieval Wall Painting* 2 vols. (New York: 1950).

28. "The American Masterpieces," *Masterpieces I* (1950), 138 ff.

29. Van Dyke, *Op. cit.* 732.

30. Margaret Brine, "Mary: Divine Shepherdess," *Perpetual Help* (March, 1951), 90-4.

31. Fernand Hazan, *Dictionary of Modern Painting* (New York: Paris: 1955) 68-70; *cfr. Herald Tribune* (December 22, 1944); *cfr.* This Week, *The Pittsburgh Press* (April 9, 1950); H. M. Gillett, *Famous Shrines of Our Lady* (Westminster, Md., 1950); *cfr.* Francis Beauchesne Thornton, *Catholic Shrines in the United States and Canada* (New York: 1953).

32. Augustine Studeny, "Babe of the Crib different from the Infant of Prague," *Narod Supplement* (January 11, 1953), with picture.

CHAPTER 2. The Holy Child of Prague

1. Is. 11:6, see Caryl Houselander, *The Passion of the Infant Christ.* (New York: 1953) 47 ff.

2. Ludvik Nemec, *The Infant of Prague* (New York: 1958) 8-15.

3. August Sedlacek, *Hardy, Zamky a tvize ceske* (Prague: 1882-1927, 15 vols.) II 202.

4. Zdenek Wirth (and associates) *Dejepis vytvernych umeni v Ceskoslovensku* (Prague: 1935) 27, 34, 56, 66, 77, 205, 318 and *passim.*

5. Marie Stechova "Duch kostela" *IPQ* 2 (1937) 106-9.

PART II

CHAPTER 3. Commentary on the Translation

1. It is in the possession of the author who provided four photostatic copies and presented them in June, 1959, to St. Procopius library, Lisle, Illinois, Library of Congress, Washington, D. C., The Catholic University of America library, Washington, D. C., and Duquesne University, Pittsburgh, Pennsylvania, in order to make this material available to the historian. A microfilm copy was presented at the same time to the Sisters of St. Joseph Archivium, Baden, Pennsylvania.

2. Anonymous, *Jashichte des gnadenreichen Prager Jebulein* (Luxemburg: 1895); 6, has his name: Nikolaus Schockweiler; likewise, one can find it in Audrey May Meyer's *The Infant King* (St. Meinrad) 15; however the majority of them: Mayer, Novotny Fontaine and *Histoire,* have Nikolaus Schokwilerg. For clarification the author wrote to Luxemburg for the baptismal certificate, but did not receive an answer.
3. First German text of Father Cyril's prayers is versified. See Emmerich, Op. cit., 6 (has 24 lines) then in Czech version of 1749.
4. This first grace given to Father Cyril by the Infant of Prague to reassure him in his religious vocation, became a cornerstone for the establishment of the patronage of Master of Vocations, which was adopted by monasteries and convents throughout the world, and where monthly novenas for vocations are held.
5. Ludvik Nemec, *The Infant of Prague* (New York: 1958) 54, 58, 60, 64, 69, 79, 82, 85, 199, 241 and *passim.*
6. Hilaire Belloc, quoted by Monsignor Ronald A. Knox "Some Problems of Bible Translation," *The Catholic Companion of the Bible.* (New York: 1956), 83.
7. James C. Carter, "The Recognition of Miracles" *Theological Studies* 20 (1959) 175-197.

REFERENCES

Part III

Chapter 6

1. The Period from Emmerich's manuscript (1737) to the expulsion of the Carmelites (1784) covers about fifty years, but from the historical aspect not too many important events took place. We may say that Emmerich's account gives an over-all picture of the period together with the help of Father John Raymund's account as mentioned in the text.
2. They are called by Father Studeny "mistaken identities," see Augustine Studeny, "The Infant of Prague and the Babe of the Crib," *The Little Flower Magazine* 37:1 (1956) 12-13, 29. *cfr.* W. Lefere "Les Statues de l'Enfant Jesus" *PR* 50 (1954) 66-69, 130-32. *cfr.* Ludvik Nemec, "Is the Infant of Prague also King of Cebu?" *Narod Supplement* (Sept. 5, 1957) 4, 10.

3. Joseph Mayer: *Milostny Jezisek V kostele Panny Marie Vitezne v Praze.* (Prague: 1884) 107. *cfr.* J. Mayer, *Op. cit.,* 107: The situation was solved in this way: The parish of Our Lady of Chains was adjoined to the territory around the Church of Our Lady of Victory and fused into one parish of Our Lady of Victory. The Carmelite Fathers were expelled on July 3, 1784 and a small annual allowance was fixed for them by the government as a substitute for the confiscation of the monastery. The number of members is known as 44, two of whom remained in the monastery to assist. *cfr.* This was called "Nabozenska Matice" which had its patronatus upon those churches and religious institutions, which were affected by the reform. *cfr.* Part of the monastery served as a school in front of which was later built the teachers' institution.

4. Bohumir Lifka, "Kazatel a farar a Jezulatka Fra Jan Raymund" *IPQ* 1 (1935) 79-83.

5. This manuscript is preserved in the parish office in Our Lady of Victory Church in Prague and in 1856 was given to the Czech Museum.

6. Artaud de Montor, *Histoire du Pope Pie VII* (3rd ed. Paris; 1839) *cfr.* Alaphridus Ottaviani, *Institutiones Juris Publica Ecclesiastice* (2 vols. 3rd. ed. Rome: 1947) *cfr. Acton, The Cambridge Moddern History* (New York: 1907) X; *cfr.* The bulls of Pius VII are partly in *Bullarii Romani continuatio* (ed. Barreri, Rome: 1846-53) vol. XI-XV.

7. He was commended for this work by Pope Leo XIII in the papal rescript of December 14, 1898.

8. *Prazske Jezulatko* (Zikes ed.) 15, *cfr.* Joseph Mayer, Op. cit., 110.

9. A few pictures of these collections are reproduced here.

10. Father Mayer used for the completion of his work, *Memorial Book,* from the parish Archives as well as those accounts contemporarily written, especially that of Father John Raymund.

11. This organization published all the books mentioned by Fontaine and serves as a center for the devotional literature and objects.

12. *The Book of Kempten* (1691)

13. Lusitanian Serbs had always maintained good relations with Prague. The clergy was educated there and all spiritual contacts were inspired there for them to maintain their own self-determination in the German atmosphere.

14. *IPQ* 1 (1935) 30; transl. from Czech; *cfr. Prva Zprava o Druzine milostneho* Prazskeho Jeziska (First report of the Sodality of the

Miraculous Infant of Prague. Prague; 1897) ; *cfr.* P. Theodore de Jesus, *Manual de la confrerie du Divin Infant Jesus of Prague.* (Lot et Garonue; 1936) .

15. *AAS* 2 (1910), *cfr. AAS* 5 (1913) 152-3, *cfr. AAS* 5 (1913), *cfr. AAS* 15 (1923) 262-3. *AAS* 11 (1920) .
16. Ludvik Nemec, *Church and State in Czechoslovakia* (New York: 1955) 96-115, *cfr. T. G. Masaryk: Los von Rom* (Boston: 1902) 16.
17. Encyclical "Quas Primas" of December 1, 1925, *AAS* 17 (1925) 598-600; *cfr.* Joseph Husslein, *Social Wellsprings* (Milwaukee: 1943) 1.
18. *Ibid.,* ES 2196.
19. Matt. 22:21.
20. Jan Karasek, *O Prazoseni Jezulatku* (Prague: 1936) Jan Karasek, *Prazske Jezulatko* (Prague: E. Beaufort 1939) .
21. V. Hellmuth Brauner "Zdenka Braunerova a Prazoke Jezulatko *IPQ* 1 (1935) 64, 86-88.
22. Henry Bordeaux, *La vie Pathetique d'Edith Stein Meditations* (Paris: La Table Ronde 1955) .
23. Gertrud von Le Fort, *Song at the Scaffold* (translated from the German by Olga Marx, New York: 1933) .
24. Cibor Moran "Apostolat Dr. Alfreda Fuchse" *Narod* (January 4, 1954) 4-6; *cfr.* Alexander Heidler, Alfred Fuchs *Novy Zivot* 6 (1956) 3-4. For his outstanding activities Dr. Alfred Fuchs was awarded the Cross of Gregory the Great by Pope Pius XI on June 30, 1936. Apostolic nuncio Monsignore S. Ritter offered personally this citation of the Pope.
25. Witnessed by many fellow prisoners.
26. Martin Turnell, "The Intolerance of Genius" *The Commonweal* 62 (May 27, 1955) 205.
27. Augustine Studeny "Paul Claudel and His L'Enfant Jesus de Prague," *Little Flower Magazine* 36: 6 (1955) 16-17, 20.
28. *Corona Benignatatis Anni Dei* (16th ed. Paris: 1915) "L'Enfant Jesus de Prague" was one of the poems included in the section "Images Saints de Boheme."
29. *The Forum,* (January 17, 1928) p. 17, 18, 20, 21, *cfr.* P. C. Woodcock, "Genius loci: *The Forum.* (August, 1928) , cfr., Sr. M. David, *America* 72 (December 23, 1944) . *cfr.* Joachim Smet, The Sword 2 (1938) .

30. Plans began early in 1927 when the Procurator General of the Order of Discalced Carmelites, Father Adeodato de S. Jose, presented his official request for spiritual benefices to the Sacred Congregation of Rites in Rome. Humbly petitioning for special indults to mark the forthcoming occasion, he requested the privilege of instituting a solemn triduum in honor of the Infant of Prague in all the churches of the Order where the Confraternity of the Infant of Prague had been canonically erected. As an added feature of the triduum, permission was asked to celebrate a votive Mass in honor of the Holy Name of Jesus. The Holy See responded favorably to the request and by rescript of the Sacred Congregation of Rites dated November 25, 1927, and the Sacred Apostolic Penitentiary Court, granted the indult requested. On December 1, of the same year, was granted a plenary indulgence to be gained on the occasion of the centenary. *cfr.* Fr. Jeronimo de Jesus "El Centenario del Nino de Praga y la Santa Sede" *El Carmelo y Praga* 12 (1928) 729-30. cfr. "El Papa y el III Centenario del Nino Jesus de Praga" *El Carmelo y Praga* 12 (1928) 929. This Spanish text comprises the contents of the respective papal decrees, quoted above. Its translation is by the author.

31. English translation from the Czech original. This pastoral letter was published as an appendix of Ordinaristne List (1933) 1; a copy of it is in the possession of the author. This pastoral letter was reprinted in many languages and appeared especially in a Spanish translation made by Professor Rudolph Sisby in *El Monte Carmelo.* 35: 598 (March, 1933) and was enthusiastically accepted. In some periodicals some parts of it were reprinted or made reference to. It may be found in L. Nemec, *Op. cit.,* 249-52.

32. *L'Osservatore Romano* (December 7, 1935) cfr. Cath. Encyc. II Suppl. 18 (1953) IV. Its brief existence was ended in 1938 during the Nazi occupation. This quarterly publication, to which reference is made with the abbreviation *IPQ* in the author's quotations, was rich with information and well-managed, reviewing history as well as recording recent happenings in different countries. It is much to be regretted that this publication did not continue after World War II (1939-45).

33. *IPQ* 1 (1935) 93-4; *cfr. Congressus Catholicus Pragensis. Prazsky Katolicky* sjezd 27-30 VI A. D. 1935. *Memoriale Illustratum.* (Prague: 1937).

34. Fra. Karel V. Horky "Vyrocni salvnost Korunovace Prazskaho Milostnaho Jezulatka dne 19. dubna 1936" IPQ 2 (1936) 20-23.

35. *IPQ* 2 (1936) 95: "La Redaccion de Ecos del Carmelo y Praga envia al Emmo Cardinal Kaspar, Arzobispo de Praga, enthusiasta felicitation por su reciente promocion al Cardenalato y dada su devotion se complace en spellidarle el Cardenal del Nino de Praga."

36. *IPQ* 3 (1937) 31 *cfr. Cath. Encyc.* II Suppl. 18 (1953) IV. cfr. Ant. Novotny, *Op. cit.,* 16. *cfr.* Dr. S. F. "Prazske Jezulatko do Argentiny *IPQ* 2 (1937) 118-119; with the accompanying pictures.

37. Father Juan Font Girald was a great patriot for the free Catalania. Former Chairman of the International Council of Catholic Esperantists and editor of Espero Katolike, he was a devout venerator of the Infant of Prague and made frequent visits to Prague to have a Mass at the altar of the Infant. He was killed in July, 1936, in the Spanish Civil War when he attempted to escape to his home in Gerona. *cfr.* IPQ. 3 (1937) 29.

38. These contents were reprinted in *IPQ* and used in various countries.

39. Very popular in Czechoslovakia and other lands on season and greeting cards.

40. Dr. Jaroslav Macha, *Modlitba za vlast k Prazskemu Jezulatku.* (Prague: 1945).

41. The paritures of this Oratorio is divided into two parts. In the present time it is in the possession of Right Reverend Monsignor Francis Planner,' Secretary of *Academia Cristiana Cecoslovacca, Via della Conciliazione, Rome.*

42. *Unto the Glory of God.* (Prague: 1955) 80, 82.

43. Brochure is in the possession of author and is illustrated with a full color picture of the Infant in His royal dress.

44. From the personal correspondence of the author. Her representation is included in one of the illustrations of this book.

45. Karel Prochazka "Medaile Prazskeho Jezulatka" *IPQ* 2 (1936), 16-19.

46. James J. Metcalfe, *Garden in My Heart.* (New York: 1949) 26.

47. The style of this poem is similar to those appearing in the Pittsburgh Post Gazette, where it portrays the deep sentiments and the right historical meaning of the Infant.

INDEX

D

E

F

G

H

I

R

S